Warm Wishes

Tony Baylon

IT'S NOT THE WINNING, IT'S THE TAKING 'APART'

A Personal Account of a Firefighter

Tony Baglow

ISBN: 978-1-4834-6338-4 (sc)
ISBN: 978-1-4834-6337-7 (e)

Lulu Publishing Services rev. date: 02/16/2017

I WOULD LIKE TO EXPRESS MY SINCERE AND SPECIAL THANKS AND GRATITUDE TO JO WHO HAS OFFERED SO MUCH SUPPORT THROUGHOUT THIS PROJECT, AND THE PATIENCE OF PUTTING UP WITH ME!!

ALSO A THANKYOU TO MY FRIENDS, THOSE WHO STILL SERVE OPERATIONALLY AND THOSE RETIRED; FOR THEIR SUPPORT AND INSPIRATION IN OFFERING ADVICE AND ENCOURAGEMENT TO INSPIRE ME TO COMPLETE THIS BOOK.

TONY BAGLOW. 2016

In 1996, there were fifty eight Fire stations throughout Devon. Eleven of these were whole-time/day-crewed stations (full-time Firefighters) and forty six stations were manned by Retained (part time) firefighters. Also a fire station manned by a volunteer crew. Retained Firefighters have other full-time occupations but they carry a bleeper/alerter which is sounded by fire control if they are required to attend an emergency call, commonly known as a *shout* within the service. To keep up to date with training the retained firefighter would have to attend drill nights at their station on a specific night of the week; also attend internal and external specialised courses as like their whole-time colleagues.

As I write, Devon fire and rescue service has now amalgamated with Somerset fire and rescue service which tallies to more appliances and personnel throughout the counties.

This book is dedicated to both sectors of the fire service of both past, present and future also including all support staff. I cover, the sometimes difficult, solemn, amusing; but overall rewarding job of the Fire service who work so hard for us, the general public, when summoned, whether they are called to a fire, a road traffic collision, a chemical incident or other special service calls. This book partially emphasises the work of road traffic collision rescue; looking at the training, the inter-fire services competitions and incidents themselves. It explains what life is like for the Firefighter from a recruit to probationer to a fully-fledged Firefighter dealing with an array of eye-opening incidents.

PROLOGUE

I am stood poised, ready for some action along with four other firefighters that are stood with me. We are all waiting for the command to 'get to work'. The scenario that is presented before us is a car which has had a head on collision with a wall, there is one person trapped in the frontal-intrusive wreckage. These incidents were called Road Traffic Accidents (RTAs) at the time. But due to legislation and mitigation of IF the unfortunate event was actually an 'accident' the term was changed to Road Traffic Collision (RTC), neutralised terminology. It is our job to extricate the casualty within twenty minutes in this scenario, the sooner and safer the better. We are five individuals who work as one, for one goal; to save life. On this hot, summers Tuesday evening I am involved in one of the many practice sessions, or drills, for us select men; as we are training for the British National Extrication Challenge -*BNEC*.

This challenge is part of the Car Users Entrapment Extrication Society-CUEES (pronounced Q. EEs). The challenge is based on a 3-tier structure, Regional, National and international competitions. We compete with other Stations to try to beat their extrication time. We also learn from each other by adapting to use different techniques to improve positions of cutting and spreading to create adequate and effective space creation and medical care.

My name is Tony Baglow, Firefighter at Station 0.2. Ilfracombe, North Devon.

Right, let's 'get to work'...............

SUMMER OF 1996

SNAP! The sound of latex medical gloves on skin is accompanied with a ghoulish low laugh as if I had just entered a horror movie starring a mad surgeon. I turn to look at my mate, the Leading Firefighter (L/FF) who had just carried out this malicious act to unnerve me. "Don't Mate I'm bloody nervous already." He just repays me with a devilish smile.

I am on my way to my first road traffic collision. Our print out sheet or 'tip sheet' from the fire station's tele- printer reveals the details of- *'Car hit wall. Person trapped'*. The Fire engine or pump as they're known to us, that I am riding; is call-sign 021, (pronounced 'Zero Two One'). It is one of two pumps that we have on station (along with a turntable ladder aerial appliance). Owing to the location of the incident being between our Town and a village called Woolacombe; fire control had sent one of our Pumps and Woolacombe's only pump, call- sign 161 ('One Six One') for a two-pump attendance. All sorts of horrific images are running through my mind regarding the incident. I don my RTC high-visibility (Hi-vis) jacket, safety glasses, fire helmet and gloves; latex medical gloves first then firefighting working gloves over the top in case I need to remove the working gloves to treat casualties. I look to my left; at least I am amongst an experienced crew. I have not been in the Service a Year yet. We take the third exit off the roundabout my nerves are really kicking in now. I am thinking through all the training that I have gained; mentally listing dangers and considerations to be aware of - slip hazards, fire, traffic control in the absence of the Police, fuel/fluid leaks, was the vehicle carrying any hazardous materials, what side of the pump the RTC kit is housed, where are the stabilisation blocks (these are wooden wedges and various-sized blocks of wood which are placed strategically under and/or around a vehicle in order to create a movement-free ridged platform. This is in case of a casualty or casualties having sustained back, neck, Cervical spine injuries in which it could be detrimental or even catastrophic to move the spinal column and cord too much as this could cause permanent paralysis.....or worse.) Then my mind mentally nudges me; the casualty; what about him or her? *Christ, I may have to deal with the casualty. Think, come on, think; first aid. Hope an Ambulance is there already.'* As we approach I see the vehicle involved, a white car, I initially did not recognise the make. To be fair who cared, I was not overly interested in that, even though it may come in handy later for knowledge of airbag or seatbelt retention systems if they needed to be isolated. My mind is churning out one hundred and one things to think of as it was. And that's not all that was churning!

As we approach I see the car is broadside across the road and partially blocking our side of the roadway so that we are presented with the nearside of the car (the passenger side). All in all it doesn't look too bad. *That's ok then, calm down.* The Ambulance was yet to turn up and still no 161 as yet. Oh bugger.

My Sub Officer (Sub O), the officer- in-charge (OIC), turns round in his seat up front and allocates jobs for the crew for when we arrived, he looks at me. "Baggy, (My nickname) I want you to stick with Jim, ok?" I acknowledge him with a quick nod, supressing my nerves "Right Sub."

We dismount from the pump when I immediately hear more sirens and take a quick glance up the road towards Woolacombe. It must be their crew on their way. I then look at the offside of the car. Ah, the car has been involved in a front quarter oblique impact with a wall, so rather than impacting head-on; the car had initially impacted the right offside front corner, this has caused immense distortion of the frame and bulkhead and some parts may have caused intrusion internally into the vehicle enough to cause injury and even trapping the occupant. We had analysed that the car had gone onto a grass verge, knocked down a four foot high wall with its front quarter, also impacting the side doors resulting in an implosion of metalwork within the vehicle itself then; bounced back onto the tarmac on all four wheels, coming to a halt partially blocking the road. Jim looks over to me. "Bags; go and have a look at the casualty mate. Check she's ok." I creep up the side of the car, still taking in the damage I draw level with the Driver's door and look in through the bent framework where the female driver is, there is no other occupants within as far as I can see. All the side glass has shattered. The young casualty is looking the other way from where I am now crouching in readiness to talk to her. All around firefighters from 021 and now 161 are bustling about the scene ascertaining where, if at all, this woman is trapped. "Hello Love, Fire Service. Could you look to your front love? As I need you to keep your head nice and straight for me. I need to check you over, to help you." She slowly turns to face me. Eyes now looking into mine, her face very bloodied; multiple lacerations; her right eye doesn't look good at all; it's almost as if the injuries to her face have distorted it. Numerous small kernels of glass in her hair are glistening in the sunlight. The glass can also be seen in her wounds. I glance quickly at the windscreen; it is cracked in a crazy pattern but no evidence of her head hitting the windscreen which would have caused a hole which would create cracks radiating out likening to a spider's web, what's known as a 'Bullseye'. She probably has hit the steering wheel with her face. No airbag deployment though. She lifts up her right hand, for reassurance rather than in offer for me to treat an injury. She looks ahead of her, very quiet, very still. I then hold her hand, and ask her a few questions. She just vaguely nods lethargically as if all the energy has drained from her.

I try and get her to speak rather than nod as to minimise neck movement. The blood; glistening red on her face is contrasted by her pale skin. More sirens are heard. *I Hope that's a bloody Ambulance.*

Jim has been over to me several times to check if I'm ok. I crack on. *Think what you need to do, THINK,* I mentally kick myself. I carry out an initial assessment on the casualty. Reflecting on these thoughts seem like a long time to think of what I needed to do and actually taking action and doing it, but in reality this was carried out in seconds under a state of calm urgency.

She probably has an injury to her oral and nasal cavities via the impact but she is making no gurgling noises, good, her airway seems patent. I can see chest rise and fall equally, she is still breathing, albeit rapidly. I feel for a pulse at the wrist, the radial pulse, I can detect that it is present but weak. I think of the secondary assessment, it now all seems to fall into place.

I feel a nudge at my left knee; I look down to see that one of the lads has slid the Manual Automatic Resuscitation System (MARS) my way. This piece of apparatus can be utilised for the unconscious victim or if they have absence of pulses, we can carry out Cardiopulmonary resuscitation (CPR) or we can administer 100% oxygen via a mask to aid breathing in cases of smoke inhalation, breathing difficulties, collapse, nausea, shock, or fluid loss and trauma. I still fire off questions to the unfortunate victim, I am still acknowledged by nods which

I try to discourage as I want to achieve audible acknowledgement from her. I compile a secondary assessment; she seems to have no obvious bone fractures or major Haemorrhage anywhere from her body. However I'm still concerned about her C-Spine. "Right listen to me, I want you to take some of this oxygen as it will do you good and clear your head a little ok?" I keep talking as I unravel the mask strap and turn on the oxygen. "You just breathe this in normally; let the oxygen do all the work ok?" I don't look at her because I want to see if I can gain an audible acknowledgement rather than a nod which I am trying to discourage. I can't get a name or any other information out of her. I just hear half-hearted grunts. That'll have to do. "Right then, someone is going to be seated behind you very soon, they will hold your head straight and very still in a neutral alignment as to protect your spine from any damage. This is all precautionary but we must do it yeah? Understand?" The reply comes in the form of another guttural grunt. "It's going to be fine, we'll look after you." I say for reassurance for her. I momentarily look up, I'm thirsty. It is a hot summer's afternoon after all. Firefighters are all over the car like bees around honey. I see the police already on scene; they've stopped the traffic and probably setting up diversions whilst we take centre stage of the whole carriageway blocking the whole road with our pumps. I see an Ambulance slowly coming to a halt. The rear door next to me has been forced open with a small tool, which is any tool that is used by hand that is not usually a power-tool; such as anything from a screwdriver to a lump hammer or a pickaxe. The door makes an unnatural creaking noise as two firefighters force it wide.

One of them slowly and cautiously, as not to make too much movement to the already stabilised car, slides into the rear seat, gets as comfortable as possible and places both his hands either side of the casualties head.

Jim is now at my side again with a cervical neck collar (C-spine collar). This device is a piece of adjustable plastic and foam with adjusters to accommodate differing neck sizes. It is in place to minimise neck movement, a 'belt-and-braces' approach that should go hand-in-hand with the use of a longboard, in order to maintain the neutral alignment of the head, neck and back.

The collar should fit quite snugly (actually- without the snugness!) around the neck. Emergency workers state that if the collar is uncomfortable then it is fitted correctly. The hands should still be applied around the outside of the C-spine collar after the collar is fitted for additional support.

The collar is duly and swiftly fitted perfectly by Jim with the assistance of the firefighter in the rear seat. I check her lower limbs, no evidence of obvious fractures but her feet look trapped in amongst the bend pedals and part of the floor pan. The ambulance crew arrive at my side. They obtain some vital clinical observations and findings from me. I am now relieved from my post as first aider/ casualty carer. The front driver's door is now forced open with the use of the small tools. The Paramedics use their more advanced medical equipment to continue to assess the casualty; next to her they place a cylinder in a blue carry bag. This cylinder contains a gas known as Entonox. It is an analgesic (pain-reliever), usually used by pregnant women during labour and can result in great pain-relieving effects. It is self-administered through a mouthpiece or facemask via a tube from the cylinder. It is then sucked into the lungs as and when required to obtain the desired effect.

I start to look around, feeling redundant, feeling quite out of place. We have the result of an RTC in front of us which I think everyone should be trying their hardest to extricate the casualty, and what am I doing?........I notice there is still debris, bits of mudguard, metal, plastic, bits of rubber and glass, still on the road at this side of the car. Thinking hazards, I walk with urgency to grab a long-handled stiff brush and return to sweep the offending wreckage remnants underneath the car. "Baggy?" The Sub officer calls. "Sub." I quickly reply. He walks briskly over to me. "Check the stabilisation again, will you?" With that, I'm onto it, checking and amending all chocks and blocks that have been selectively placed round all four wheels. I make amendments to a few loose ones in some stacks but the others remain tight and stable. Chocks can move and work loose through transmitted movement caused by weight-shift such as someone getting into the vehicle to carry out some work or one of the casualties being removed first, also cutting and removing bits of metal, such as removing the roof can all cause destabilisation. On occasions the chocks and blocks maybe accidently be kicked or nudged as rescue workers go about their work.

Stabilisation should be checked and re-checked at regular times throughout the rescue. I confirm that this task is complete then continue to clear debris and head back to the casualty.

I am getting quietly frustrated. In my mind I am shouting '*Why haven't we got her out by now?*' I see the driver's door now fully opened and tied back with a line (rope) to the axle for safety.

Owing to this being an RTC I am now expecting the big 'Hurst' 'Jaws of life' hydraulic power cutters and spreaders to come into play, they have been set up at the equipment area in readiness of their marvellous power to create space; but Instead I see a toolbox brought to the driver's door. *Eh?* The Ambulance crew suggest that we need not cut and remove the roof but suggested that we get her out of this side door onto a longboard, which is a hard flat board which accompanies the C-spine collar to immobilise the casualty. I see one of Ambulance crew fetching their wheeled stretcher with the longboard on top assisted by a firefighter from 161's crew. They place the stretcher near the driver's door in preparation to receive the casualty once removed. Mike and Jim are kneeling down, craning their bodies looking down into the footwell. The seat has managed to be forced back on its runners. There seems no obvious intrusion from the bulkhead trapping the woman. Jim looks up "Bag's, pass us a spare hacksaw blade out of the toolbox will you?" I oblige. "The pedals have bent round and trapped her feet. We're not going to relocate the pedals easily; we'll need to cut the pedal stems." Jim says just loud enough for me to hear. We didn't have such a tool as a pedal cutter in North Division at the time; and we couldn't get the whole hacksaw handle in the footwell. I was just about to ask the question of what I can do; when Jim, without looking round, says "You can get in here in minute bags and take over." Finally some rescue work, albeit with a hacksaw blade and no hydraulic power-tool giants to play with. I'm now sawing away on the brake pedal, which oddly resembles an open ivy vine spiralling around a tree. I couldn't help but think what a strange abstract, even ornate, shape that pedal had taken on through just a single impact. These pedal stems are harder than you think. Sweat now dripping from my chin in this confined distorted space, breathing heavy as I furiously saw through the metal to release the woman's foot from the clutches of this wreckage. Mike shouts down "Alright bags? Need to change over?" I keep sawing with urgency "Nope, I'm alright ta" I say with newly keen eagerness. I continue a few seconds more, I'm through. Phew. I then go to start on the clutch pedal, when I feel a tap on the back The Leading Firefighter looks down at me "That'll do mate, I'll get in there, go have a cool down. Well done." I undo the Velcro fastening of my high visibility jacket, but as procedure, I keep it on. I remove my helmet as I am away from the rescue work and walk toward the grass verge and suck in the welcome breeze. My whole body is sweating. I've not even done much, had anyone really? I grab a few bottles of water that have been brought out early on and I pass a couple out to other now 'redundant' fire crews awaiting further instructions.

The trapped casualty is now free. We all help out to assist the Ambulance crew manoeuvre her onto the longboard then into the Ambulance. I go back to have a quick survey of the now empty wreck of the car. The Leading Firefighter comes over and administered an over enthusiastic back-slap. "Well done mate on your first one."

I still feel that I didn't actually do much to contribute; it certainly feels like I should have done more. Probably my probationary naivety expectations deluded me that every RTC we attend we NEED TO get the powerful hydraulic *Jaws of Life* to work, and that at every RTC we HAVE TO cut the roof off and every RTC HAS TO be catastrophic for us, the Fire Service.....How wrong could I be.

THE BEGINNING

F rom the age of five I knew that I wanted to be a Fireman. It was probably the fire engine that went roaring up that London Street in which I spent a few years of my life with my Family in the capital. The fire engine was on an emergency call with its blue roof beacons flashing and bell ringing as this was the main audible method back in 1975; the appliance looked spotless and very smart as it went past me with urgency with its *'London fire brigade'* livery emblazoned proudly upon its panelling. I stood in awe wondering where the crew were going; conjuring up all imaginative incidents in my mind; could they be pulling some unfortunate person from the clutches of a ravaging fire, cutting people out of a car crash, dealing with leaking chemicals, investigating a fire alarm that had been actuated, it really piqued my interest and rather than a gradually fading interest the feeling of being a fireman bore stronger and stronger.........

During that year of 1975 my family and I moved to the coastal town of Ilfracombe in North Devon in which I attend three schools with the image of a future career with the fire service still planted deep in my mind. In my last two years of comprehensive school I worked part-time after school in a local store, where I would stack shelves for some extra money. The local fire station was located just a little way from the store. Every Tuesday evening the local retained (part-time firemen) conducted a two-hour drill session from, 7pm until 9pm, in order to practice and hone their skills. So, when I finished stacking the shelves in the store at 7pm I would buy myself a drink and some 'munchies' and walk up to the car park next to the fire station and watch spectacular drills unfold. Ladders would be pitched to the high drill tower, jets of water from various sized hoses would be trained on an imaginary fire emitting from the façade of the third floor of the tower and Firemen were putting on their cumbersome breathing apparatus sets (BA) in readiness to fight the through the cumbersome hindering smoke. It was all very exciting for a young lad who could imagine himself in that drill yard, wearing that uniform, doing that job that he dreamed of.

Some nights they would use large special cutting and spreading tools to cut open a wrecked car to simulate extracting and rescuing trapped casualties. I could not really see what was going on with the drill as there were a sea of yellow fire-helmets surrounding the car as the crews worked on it so intently. Some nights I was unlucky as when I arrived at the car park the drill yard, down below, was in darkness but lights were on upstairs in the fire station indicating that they were probably having an operational lecture on one subject or another or the crews would, on some occasions, go out somewhere in town for off-station drills or exercises.

One particular night a leading fireman, Steve Mcgovern, spotted me supping my drink and alerted my presence to the rest of the lads who turned to look at me quickly before looking away again. Steve said that he knew me, "He's keen you know, he's going to be a fireman one day, you watch" Steve said to them. The next week a car was being cut up again, this time the Sub officer, Terry Derrin, spotted me for the umpteenth time and waved me over to the drill yard, I actually looked over my shoulder to see if he was summoning someone else. "Me?" I mouthed whilst actually pointing to myself. Terry nodded with a smile so I eagerly hopped over the small wire fence and headed over to where the fire crews were professionally dismantling this car. As the crews worked feverishly on the car a firefighter approached me and nodded to them "I love seeing the kids playing with these toys." I stayed and watched in awe as they dismantled this vehicle with an urgent purpose.

"What are you doing next Tuesday evening Tony?" The Sub O was now beside me.

"Ugh, um, nothing. Why's that then?" I said.

The Sub O continued to shout through the resounding noise in the drill ground. "Be up here for about twenty past seven next Tuesday, you could help us in a BA exercise, we could do with another casualty. You up for it?" I was over the moon and gratefully accepted the invite to participate.

I arrived at the station five minutes earlier than the designated time. The crews had just finished parade or roll call which is carried out at the commencement of the drill session or shift to officially ascertain who is in attendance; and to allocate the jobs that they would be doing on the fire appliances, this has stemmed from a long tradition. The crews had also been briefed as regards to the evening's exercise which was to be a BA search and rescue with me playing one of the starring roles.

Terry sent both appliances up the road, out of the way, as we placed rescue dummies at strategic and awkward places throughout. He then turned to me and threw me an old fire tunic and leggings; complete with a smoky aroma. "Put that on mate and follow me," I was to wear this in order to keep my own clothes clean for when I am 'rescued' and dragged out. Terry had already fast tracked through two sets of doors which passed through a room which contained fire kit, known as the Muster bay, which in turn led into the appliance bay; now void of the pumps apart from the turntable ladder appliance, which still resided at Ilfracombe fire station until it permanently relocated to Barnstaple fire station in 1996 – the year that I was destined to join.

I eventually caught up with the Sub O who was waiting by a recess in the corner of the room which housed some stores, cleaning products and other such-like consumables, the recess had no door and measured approximately six feet by six feet.

Terry pointed to a corner of the recess "There you go Tony, pop yourself on the floor in the corner, keep quiet, act unconscious and let them do what they're trained to do ok?"

"Right ok." I said as I cautiously slumped in the corner, feeling a little nervous about the whole scenario. Terry started talking into a hand-held radio as he was walking away. Within two minutes I heard the sound of air brakes outside the station then doors slamming and the leading firefighters (L/FFs) shouting orders as the exercise started to unfold.

Within another minute I heard the main front door of the fire station being opened and slammed back against the stopper on the wall as if opened in anger. Although they were quite a way from my location I could hear the muffled voices of the BA wearers as they were communicating with each other; the leading person feeding back information such as left and right turns, low ceilings, obstructions, doors. This had to be the way to communicate as the BA crews wore opaque sticky visors that can be temporarily fit over the face mask to mimic a very smoky environment for exercise purposes; so everything is located by touch as they both searched. "BA CONTROL (BACO) FROM BA TEAM 1. CASUALTY LOCATED AT FOOT OF STAIRS, WITHDRAWING WITH CASUALTY OVER."

I heard another team searching the station, they came through the first far door leading into the muster bay. I could hear the muffled sounds of their voices through the facemask a likening to the star wars character Darth Vader. I could hear their boots tap against the wall in the room next to me as they were feeling the floor for obstructions and casualties as they went. The second door that led to the appliance bay then swung back and I could hear the crews clearer as they approached my location. I was quite excited whilst awaiting the prospect of 'rescue', this was fine in training but would never like to be in a situation where I had to be rescued in this particular predicament for real. The BA crews drew nearer; "TURNING LEFT, OBSTRUCTION LOW DOWN ON THE LEFT, WATCH THE CABLE." The team was right at the entrance to the room where I was 'unconscious' but I had not seen them yet through half opened eyes, but I knew it would be seconds. A hand gripped the opening to the room. "OPENING ON THE LEFT, ENTERING THE..............OH BUGGER! HERE WE GO!"

All the lights came on in the station and the sound of the call out warblers resounded their two-tone urgency around the station. The BA team had now disappeared as I quickly opened my eyes to another drama - a real emergency call mid-exercise. I stood up and peered around the corner the station was empty once again apart from the remaining 'casualties', myself and the Sub O.

The warblers stopped sounding in replacement of two sets of two-tone horns as both pumps headed off down the road on another mission. Terry came to find me to say that they were responding a fire alarm that had actuated and a smell of burning at a property.

So, I was that close to being 'rescued'; I was slightly disappointed that I had not experienced it in this scenario, but also slightly relieved. It goes to show that an emergency can crop up at any time whatever is happening.

BRITISH NATIONAL EXTRICATION SOCIETY – BNEC

Many of the Brigades in the UK were not run by fire authorities until the 1980's as they remained under local County Council's jurisdiction. Devon Fire Brigade was governed by Devon County Council. Historically, before the 1950's, the Fire Service, nationally was not solely responsible for extricating crash victims from wrecked vehicles. They had no statutory duty to attend any road or rail accidents. They were not equipped or even trained in such a specialist task. Garage mechanics and breakdown recovery staff that were located next to busy main roads used to be first at the scene of an RTC. If persons were trapped in the wreckage then it would be these who would extricate those casualties by using various items of vehicle repair and recovery equipment, such as, winches, block and tackle gear, hacksaws and other small tools, such as small spreaders and rams, which were hand operated by hand or foot pump, also pneumatic tools namely, cengar saws and chisel/zip guns which were run off compressed air.

In the book, '*RESCUE- The history of the Britain's Emergency services' By Gavin Weightman*, it is stated that in 1955 a Gentleman who owned a local garage close to the A1 in Yorkshire used to be alerted to the sound of a collision and went to see if he could assist in anyway. Sometimes the local Police would call him up at night to summon him to bring his recovery lorry and equipment to the scene of a crash nearby to help. It is mentioned that the village of Catterick was one of the worst black spots, notorious for road collisions. In the Catterick area there were reports of one fatal collision amongst twenty nine accidents in a six month period. Due to this increase in accidents resulting in massive carnage on this road attempts were made to provide an urgent rapid response; to save lives by equipping emergency services with some form of cutting equipment. Also before this period the emergency services carried next to nothing, only small tools for other 'special service calls'.

Today, the Fire Service still have evidence on the pumps of the days when the rescue work was undertaken by the local garages. The cengar saw, chisel/zip gun and 'epco' spreading and ramming bars. These are Bars of different lengths which are linked by threaded collets and used to shore-up or push material apart, a hydraulically hand-operated pump is used to extend the bars, and this is very effective and very quiet. They are still seen on pumps in Devon and still used (at the time of writing) these all stemmed from the garage trade. It is impressive that these rescue tools work hand - in - hand with the hydraulic power cutters and spreaders that would eventually superseded this original equipment.

Early in 1997 a team was devised at Ilfracombe to become the RTC challenge team, purely for competition purposes as part of the CUEES. We were representing Ilfracombe Fire Station. The other team in North Devon also representing the area at the time; were stationed at North Tawton, near Okehampton.

Our team is comprised of:

STATION OFFICER: Phil Golding – Overall team manager/Advisor (our ambassador).

STATION OFFICER: Roy Hale- Team manager/advisor.

SUB OFFICER: Ben Williams – Officer in Charge (doesn't have to be an operational officer to be an OIC of a competing team).

SUB OFFICER: Terry Derrin – Toolman - Operates the hydraulic cutting and spreading equipment also using small tools for space creation to extricate casualties.

FIREFIGHTER: Tony Baglow – Toolman – Operates the hydraulic cutting and spreading equipment also using small tools for space creation to extricate casualties.

LEADING FIREFIGHTER: Jim Stone - Medic. Self- explanatory.

FIREFIGHTER: Mike Holt - Second Medic

The first Regional challenge had been planned for the 5th October 1997. It was to be held at the Devon Fire and Rescue Service Headquarters (SHQ), Glen Road, Plymouth in West Devon. This establishment is where all Wholetime recruits and Retained recruit Firefighters come to achieve the arduous recruit's course before being passed out (Sometimes literally) to be posted to their respected stations. Attached to the SHQ is Plympton Fire Station.

As a team we trained frequently in our spare time and very intensely prior to the build up for a challenge. Please bear in mind that being part of the team made us no way superior or specially advanced in rescue techniques than any other serving Firefighters. We were merely selected or opted to be part of the team. We wanted to represent our area. So one Saturday morning the team assembled, loaded the Fire station's personnel vehicle and headed down to Brigade Headquarters. We took our firefighting uniform, or fire kit as it is known, and any other small bits and bobs to assist us with the scenarios that the organising and judging team could throw at us.

It was the usual banter and chat on the way to Plymouth. On arrival we rendezvoused with the safety guys who gave us the low-down on all safety matters for the day. A few of us were browsing through programme of the day entitled, '**It's not the winning it's the taking apart'**, as is the title of this book. I thought it very clever wording for RTC work but we were aiming to be winners, professionals at competitions and real incidents. We were then told where we would come in the pecking order. We were team four. So we, and other teams, headed up to the viewing gallery which overlooked the drill ground which was centre stage for the onslaught of the challenge. It sent shivers down my spine to look down on that drill ground again just thinking that a couple of years ago myself and a few other recruits were getting shouted and bawled at for messing up yet another drill and quips of "Come on shift your arses, get that hydrant open, get up that ladder; The glamour model Claudia Schieffer's up there and needs rescuing, Move, move! Come on hurry up." Anyway, back to the day. General chat transformed into chat about the RTC scenarios. "Hope the first team gets a car on its roof or on its side" I said to no one in particular. And the reason I had said this? Well, we trained with cars that ended up at all sorts of angles that were very trying for crews. Safety to the fire crews is paramount. When cars ended up on their roofs we would have to go about stabilising it by positioning chocks and blocks between the windscreen, in front of the two windscreen pillars, the 'A' posts, where the front of the wing meets the ground. We then would have to stabilise the rear of the vehicle by chocks at the lowest point which was usually sufficient for holding a hatchback car but if we had a saloon with a boot, we may have to use the boot to stabilise it by using foam canisters and/or rolled hose to fill the gap to stabilise it. This can be fiddly at times but was normally straight forward. Now, for the vehicle on its side, no one really relished this scenario. We had to, again, chock the lower gaps under the A post, B-post (middle) and C-post (post behind rear door). Due to not wanting the car to destabilise and tip over, which isn't a clever situation, we would have to prevent this by using a short extension ladder which was split into two sections and used under the uppermost wheels to the ground and anchored with a rescue line to stabilise it from tipping over, (Nowadays ratchet straps are used in conjunction with the split ladder sections and vehicle and sometimes mechanical rams). This sounds quite quick, reading about this technique, but this can be fiddly and time consuming, especially when you only have twenty minutes maximum to get the casualty free. Remember, safety first. The vehicle on all four wheels - BONUS. Chock and block the wheels, block under four points under the sills - job done; now onto the glass management and metal cutting.

The organisers probably picked scenarios randomly, probably a scenario picked out of a hat along with a team number. But went on the chances of probability.

First team - Car on its side. Excellent - May reduce our chances of getting this scenario.
Second team - Car on its roof - Nice one.
Third team - Car on all fours - NO!
Fourth team.............
We we're called to the equipment area (all extrication gear provided

by Service HQ) to select and check what kit we wanted to use and to show the organisers what extra kit we may have brought with us so it could be adjudicated to make sure there was no cheating. After the checks we then donned our fire kit and lined up to await our fate.

We had the car on its roof. Oh well, could have been worse, could have been on its side. We were called into the arena, we jogged in as a team with fresh keenness. Carrying the first aid kit Jim immediately attended to lone casualty, the driver, who was hanging by his seatbelt (when situations permits all 'casualties' were 'live', not training dummies). Jim was joined by Mike accompanied with the 'MARS' resuscitation equipment, they both started dealing with the driver; we had been told that he was not physically trapped but would be in need of rapid extrication onto a longboard owing to the mechanism of injury due to the rollover of the vehicle. Terry and I got to work stabilising the vehicle to eliminate any movement even spinning seeing that it was resting on its metal roof on the concrete surface. The two medics got to work assessing and treating accordingly sprinkled with bouts of reassurance. They were also under the watchful eyes of the medic judges. Ben had now made an overall assessment of the scene and had allowed for any fuel and fluid spillages to be taken care of along with debris and fire risk (there was none obvious). He liaised with the medics who advised that the casualty was conscious and breathing but had severe upper back pain and should come out in the straightest fashion possible. It would had been ideal to lower the victim in a controlled manner onto a board which was placed and secured with the foot of the board just inside the driver's door; so that the casualty could be brought out this way. This situation was far too risky for any slight twisting of the torso. Ben turned to me and Terry. "Right Gents, all stabilised?" "All done" We acknowledged.

We were starting to perspire already due to the sun's heat and heavy fire kit. Ben pointed to the rear window of the hatchback "OK the task is a straight forward extrication. I want you to pop the rear window out, check stabilisation, one of you climb in, the other check for movement again, and pass a longboard in through the back also assist Jim and Mike with the controlled extrication of the casualty... we'll bring him back through the car and out to a place of safety to await further medical attention. Clear?" We nodded then got to work stripping the rubber that secured the rear glass screen in place within the metal bodywork then we offered up a screwdriver into the groove that was now exposed, removing the rubber and literally popping the glass out as one piece; very easy on an old make of car.

Mike had already placed a cervical collar on the casualty which made me grin with admiration of the bloke's skills to perform such a task upside down, as this can sometimes be tricky to perform on someone the correct way round. We all physically supported the casualty as not to let him drop on us or the longboard in a messy heap. I thought marks would be deducted for that don't you think?!

So we all braced up around the casualty. The seatbelt was cut through, the victim gently lowered and placed on the longboard and slid carefully back in a controlled manner on the internal roof of the car whilst trying not to drip sweat on the poor guy at this point. Once out of the vehicle we began to gather the straps and headblocks so that we could secure the driver on the board. We didn't get that far. The whistle sounded to indicate the end of the scenario. We had done well. The casualty was placed on the ground just shy of the twenty minute mark.

Vehicles on their sides or on their roofs mainly posed difficulties and unique challenges for firefighters when it came to rapid but safe extraction. We were usually governed by the Ambulance service as regards to any medical aspect as they can recognise issues that we cannot always see. At the crash scene we tell the Paramedics what we can do (usually anything and everything as regards to extrication) and ask them what they would like us to do, they tell us, and we get on with it. If the casualty has back pain or has rolled their vehicle but has no other injuries apart from a few cuts and bruises, then the Paramedics will describe the casualty as 'little sick' (so, they're not *overly* worried as regards to their condition and /or injuries....so far.) So we have good time for cutting metal and removing the roof or side door at a more relaxed controlled safe pace albeit still with urgency; but. However, if that victim has a massive internal haemorrhage has difficulty breathing, heart complications, punctured lung or lungs, major head and/or brain injury, long bone fractures which may cause internal catastrophic bleeding......you get the idea, that casualty is then described as 'big sick'. This is from the time we arrive on scene to start work when they're big sick or rapidly deteriorate during extrication. The Paramedics will probably then say to us that we should just get them out by any means. If we don't get them out very soon then they could deteriorate further or even die.

So we have to abandon our original idea of roof removal and other procedural techniques and get them out of a gap created previously, such as out through the side door.

Back in the drill yard in Plympton we thankfully removed our fire helmets, protective goggles and fire tunics in the replacement of fresh air and a nice mellow cool breeze. Cold bottled water was guzzled down the throat with haste and the last remaining splash was allowed to run over our heads to emphasise the cooling effect. We all congratulated ourselves quietly and followed a judge to a room for the debrief session. We done well, accumulated good points. We then popped up to the viewing galley to watch the remainder of the teams. One team with a car on all fours scenario had just finished their task.

North Tawton's team were just limbering up for their challenge, car on its roof also. They went on to do very well also with the casualty extricated on the whistle. With all the teams now completed their challenges we learned that we have come joint-first place with North Tawton to represent the Brigade in the National event of this year at Manchester where the BNEC would take place at Thompson Street Fire Station. We received our trophies, certificates. Lots of back slaps then home for tea and medals. Hoorah!

THE FIRST CALLS

Ilfracombe Fire Station, at the time, was made up of Whole-time (full-time) Firefighters and retained (Part-time) Firefighters. The Whole-time personnel covered days only at Ilfracombe; so they were known as the 'Day-crew'. Nights and weekends (day and night) were covered by the retained crews. If a shout came in on a weekday; the retained would cover 022. Overall we had sufficient cover 24/7. 365 days of the year. Most stations in Devon were made up of retained crews; this was due to the locality in the rural area where calls may not be so numerous to warrant a whole-time crew to man a station.

My first three emergency calls did not actually involve fire at all. We were on station, on a drill night having just finished our recruit assessment, assessed by Station officer Golding. He had just signed our paperwork and passed us as competent to ride the pumps. He had just finished the paperwork; and then it happened. Just after 9pm the station 'system' sounded (the two-tone warblers which alert everyone to an emergency call.) I was sat in the lecture room upstairs with the other three probationary Firefighters. Sub officer Derrin had made a hasty exit and ran out of the lecture room and joined the other Firefighters that were jogging down the stairs (there was (and still is) no fireman's pole at Ilfracombe Station.) Me and the other three 'probies' just looked at each other "Can we go? Do we have to stay?" we asked confusingly. A voice boomed up from the bottom of the stairs "Come on you lot, get down here, shift your arses." The voice of the Sub echoed on. Again we all looked at each other with mixed feelings of excitement and anticipation as we clumsily fed our way through the chairs that had been abandoned from the lecture session earlier in the evening. I reached for my fire kit and donned it a little too hastily as I made a hash of finding the sleeve opening of my tunic; I then was not able to marry up the zip mechanism due to shaky hands. As we entered the appliance bay I noticed a red and green light illuminated on the ceiling above both pumps respectively, these indicated that both fire engines were required. I didn't know what the shout (Incident) involved or even where we were going? I was just about to climb aboard the first pump, 021 only to be grabbed by an experienced firefighter and removed from the pump. This was the duty 'fireman's' position on the first pump. "My seat matey" he said to me and pointed to the second appliance, 022. I shrugged my shoulders "Sorry mate." I jogged across to 022 where I was 'helped' (manhandled) aboard by grabbing hands, then bundled into the middle and plonked myself down next to another proby who had found his way onto the pump with glee. I looked across back to 021 as it headed off into the night; lights flashing, engine revving, sirens trumpeting their urgent chorus. We followed in the same manner. Sirens then sounded as we approached the high street.

The firefighter on my left was booking out the appliance over the main-scheme radio to our control, based in Exeter; some fifty five miles away. "What is it?" Where are we going?" I asked the guy next to me; it transpired that we were off to a local nursing home.

He turned to me again and gently nudged me "AFA" he shouted over the roar on the engine and the two-tone siren. "Huh?" I said with

misplaced eagerness. "An A.F.A. - Automatic Fire Alarm sounding."
We turned into the nursing home's driveway. I saw the guys on 021
dismounting. I shouted over to the Sub officer sat in the front as if
to prompt him with a reminder that he actually had two probies to
contend with. He quickly looked back in response to the prompt. He
pointed to my mate first "You go with him, and baggy you go with
him". He pointed with his instructions "All of you with me first and
we'll check the Fire alarm panel then I will task you from there." A red
light was flashing at 'Zone 2' on the panel; which indicated that the
detector that had been actuated was located on the first floor, maybe
in the main corridor or in one of the resident's rooms. But what had
triggered it? We were then tasked, so we joined a few of the lads and
started to search the first floor from the opposite end, we carried
torches and radios with us. We had been searching for the culprit
detector for about two minutes when a voice crackled over the radio.
"Got it Terry, Room 25, Looks like steam from a kettle has triggered
the alarm." We continued with the floor search as to confirm there
was definitely no fire situation, and all was confirmed safe within
five minutes. The alarm then reset, staff advised, control informed,
job done. We headed back to station. I removed my fire helmet and
realise that my hands were still shaking. The call-out alerters did not
sound again for the rest of the night. My second shout, the next day,
was to a local house to aid a young girl who had accidently locked
herself in the bathroom. With some hand tools we managed to gain
access and let her out and returned to a frantic mother. My third shout
was to a person shut in a lift at our local Hospital. Again, lift keys,
small tools and the location of the elevator's motor room was needed
to release the person.

My first actual fire was at around Seven o'clock one summer's
evening. 022 headed out the doors with a full crew of six, which
consisted of four firefighters in the back and the officer in charge

(OIC) and obviously the driver in the front. We were responding to reports of smoke on some waste ground to the side of a local factory. Upon our arrival there was a patch of vegetation smouldering merrily with the minor appearances of tongues of flame every so often in the thick undergrowth. The area involved was approximately 20ft x 10ft. It wasn't the most mammoth of fires. Sub officer Williams tasked me along with another Firefighter to grab a long-handled fork and a 'grab-fork' in order to turn over and pull apart the smouldering vegetation so as to allow another of the crew to use the hosereel tubing to extinguish the fire deep at its base. Once we had turned over and given the area a good 'drink' to quench the fire within we headed back to station, cleaned the pump and re-filled the pump's water tank via the hydrant.

We hadn't used a lot of water but if we needed to use more, we would have had to connect into a fire hydrant to supplement the pump's water tank supply. The Dennis RS pump held 1800 litres (400 gallons) of water. If we used a large fire hose (a main jet) or even two hosereels at high pressure then the tank would realistically last anything from twenty minutes to two minutes.

Throughout the summer we had attended quite a few jobs, namely car fires, AFA's, RTC's (including the RTC mentioned in the prologue), people locked inside vehicles and property, people locked out of property, property fires, bin fires/rubbish fires, grass/gorse fires, barn fires, thatched roof fires, flooding, chemical incidents.... you name it we attended it.

APRIL 1996 – RECRUIT BASIC TRAINING

T en new recruits were to meet up at the Service Training Centre at Plympton, Plymouth for the commencement of the fire service basic training course. Anyone who has been in the forces; think back to your arrival and the start of your training under the bawling instructors...............thought back? Right, that's what it was like. The Fire Service is a much disciplined service and lives up to that. Four of us from my station jumped off the mini-bus with all our brand new unblemished shiny kit in tow. One of the lads, Mick, spotted a staff member (thankfully not an instructor) "Here mate, where can we get a brew round here?" he asked with ease. The staff member turned slowly around to face him then laughed to himself "Bloody hell, asking for a cuppa as soon as you show up? You'll make a bloody good Fireman!" he pointed to the side of the building "In through those doors, past reception, take the first flight of stairs up to the first floor then turn left. Canteen right in front of you" he then walked off still chuckling to himself. "Christ that sounded like an advanced BA search brief already." I said as we walked off in search of a brew. The canteen was huge. I suppose it had to be; given that it was home to Whole-time and Retained recruits alike. In-keeping with the Fire service, there were red chairs; red tiles in the kitchen area, even the horizontal Venetian window blinds were red. In the corridors there were many large glossy pictures proudly in their frames denoting various aspects of what the Fire Service carry out when summoned. Black and white prints of the old Plymouth brigade. Modern aspects of training life such as ladder work, breathing apparatus training in fire situations, chemical incident training all boasted this venture's challenges; an exciting insight of the work that we will be doing alongside those who are already doing it.......if we passed this course.

Back to Mick quickly, He and his fiancée married in 2001; in which I was delighted to be asked to perform the duties of best-man. Oh what a stag night! For the big day a fire service theme seemed appropriate as I was informed by Mick. So the firefighters that attended the wedding wore the traditional 'fireman's uniform' for ceremonial occasions, black uniform in contrast with white gloves and white belts completed with shiny hand held axes. That was the attire of the day. They formed the perfect guard of honour which led from the church doors extending toward an old lynch gate, all axes raised and angled inward to form the apex of the arch as the happy couple blissfully walked beneath it. Before the ceremony the bride-to-be arrived on time! And her carriage was a Dennis R.S. Series fire engine, the same ones that we trained with and that were still operational at the time. The appliance was festooned with ribbons and bows and chauffeured by the Divisional Officer in a fitting sense of ceremony.

The big day went extremely well and was blessed with plenty of sunshine. Mick and I trained together along with the other probationary firefighters. He went on to accomplish twenty years of dedicated service with Devon and Somerset Fire and Rescue Service.

On the first day at training school the staff talked about

Brigade-orientated subjects such as, rules and regulations, ranks and rank markings and how to recognise them, dangers, our time here, all followed by a wonderful three hour health and safety lecture. Now that really piqued my interest......to fall asleep (I never though!) We didn't talk much about breathing apparatus as that was a separate specialised course in which we would undertake at Exeter after the completion of basic training. We did have plenty of time in the afternoon to learn about the knots that the fire service uses in certain situations and discussed the dangers that could be all to present in the job.

On changing into fire kit in the changing rooms one of the lads from another station came storming in "Bloody hell. This job is dangerous 'aint it? I only joined because the missus liked the uniform." This was followed by the rapturous laughter from all present.

Second day we were introduced to ladders. Hello ladders! The main ladders on a pump comprised of a 1.3.5. Ladder (50 foot), 1.0.5. Ladder (30ft), a short-extension ladder (or first floor ladder) and a roof ladder to be slid up an angled roof assisted by small wheels then flipped over which allowed a large hook to be held onto the other side of the roof, over the ridge tiles. We practiced a couple of times with the latter two ladders as they were straight forward to use. Now, the former two were a little bit more complicated until you got the general gist of it. The Instructors demonstrated the use of the main 1.3.5. Ladder and got four of us to go through it at slow time. Putting this beast up required absolute team-work. If you're not willing to play ball and do your part properly, the thing won't be going up, simple as that, and things can go wrong. Lots of shouting instructions were required by the ladder crew to manoeuvre this heavy long piece of kit. If a foot is not placed down on the beam at the bottom of this ladder to keep the weight on, or is taken off at the wrong time then the ladder could easily 'walk' and then fall down. It had happened in the past so we were told by firefighters back on station. When we eventually got the hang of pitching the ladder we had to do it again, then again and again and several more times; then at a faster pace which was increased the more we did it. If we messed up, we were told to pitch it again. All the time the instructors were bawling at us with illusions that there was some beautiful model that needed rescuing from the floors above us. The mind is a wonderful thing and the imagination was made to run wild. It worked! Great ladder pitches followed. Other technical pitches were learnt like the bridging pitch and confined-space pitch, but I'll save you from the technicalities of these pitches!

When we removed the ladder off a fire engine and placed it up against the building this was known as the 'slip and pitch' we *slipped* the ladder from the appliance and *pitched* it to the building. The four of us from our station had a sneaky 10 hour training session on the weekend prior to the course (split 5 hours a day) to give us a 'heads-up' on what to expect and to make us shine a little, of course.

During those 10 hours of hose running and ladder pitches at our station we were taught to shout the order of 'PREPARE TO SLIP' as we ran towards the pump, then shouted 'SLIP' when we were in the process of removing it from its gantry. So at the Service training centre we used the order '*Prepare to slip*' only to be stopped abruptly by the Station officer instructor immediately. "Whoa, Whoa, Whoa, the order is '**STANDBY** to slip', **STANDBY**. Got it?"

This may sound a little finicky and pedantic to the reader but as mentioned this is a disciplined service and these orders had been used for years. Also we needed to 'play the game.' In addition to this if a firefighter shouted another order on the fire-ground that was alien or not recognised or understood then this could lead to questioning, confusion and as a result - delays. The Station officer went into a bit of a grilling session before we were told to carry on. One of the lads shouted out the order "PREPA......STANDBY TO SLIP". As I waited for the ladder to come off I glanced at the Station officer as he had not stopped us, he nodded his head and said in a - '*I just want to give up*' manner. "Carry on." After the drill, which went quite well, the Station officer came over to the appliance where we were smartly fell in. "That wasn't a bad effort" I was thinking great, give us a break, get this heavy kit off and grab a brew, he then continued "We're going to do that drill again" I gritted my teeth and thought what he had just said; **We're** going to do that drill again?' you're not mate your just going to stand there in your white helmet and shout and bawl orders at us. The Instructor continued "So same drill again and this time YOU PREPARE FUCK ALL!" You hear?" We all shouted at once in response "Yes Sir." He swapped us around by one position and scanned the line "CREW, GET TO WORK."

Hose running was not that popular an aspect in the fire service, especially when you have just run out the first four 75ft long 70mm hoses at breakneck speed and didn't pace yourself; then learned that you have to run out another six of them. Making them up was a bit awkward too, you had to crouch down very low or kneel to start to roll them in a tight turn and as the hose roll got bigger and higher you were then in an arched-bent over type of position then up to a general bending position until the hose was rolled completely. You're back used to ache after a morning session of that. We then learned about the intricacies and science of hydraulics on how to 'lift' water with the pump, the use of a small portable pump in which four firefighters could carry to a water source and lift water up to a jet or a pumping appliance; this was called the Light Portable Pump (LPP) which actually there was nothing light or really portable about it.

The old Godiva LPP was like shunting a car engine about, especially when you had to get it down a narrow bumpy track or grass riverside bank. The next two days, more of the same; ladders in the morning and hose and pump work in the afternoon then being introduced to the ever loyal fire hydrant. Overall, I was enjoying the training (despite the inward moaning) it was new, refreshing and interesting and would stand me in good stead in the future. On the Thursday morning we were all lined up in fire kit order outside our block and whilst talking to each other we stared at a bin full of cut sections of lines (ropes) in front of us.

We thought nothing of them as we carried on gassing to one and other. The Instructors could leave us standing out there for a long time if they wanted to. A whisper was passed up from one end of the line of recruit firefighters and ended up at the other end of the line very quickly. "Watch out, he's up at the office window." One by one we looked up and saw one of the instructors holding a mug of steaming hot tea as he watched us from above. He glared at us then to the bin and back to us again. Someone cottoned on to what he wanted us to do so this recruit firefighter walked over to the bin picked out a length of line and started to practice some knots. Another followed suit, then I grabbed a piece and started practicing, all of us were now practicing knots, the talking had stopped and I took a sneaky glance up at the office window again, he had gone. Five minutes later the fire-kitted forms of the Station officer, and other Instructors, walked up to the motley crew in front of them; in which we were now furiously concentrating on the knots and line work. One of the Sub Officers stopped our practice session and called us to the attention. "I am glad you now realise that when you wait for the training staff then YOU DO SOMETHING. The clue was in that bin there." he said whilst he casually nodded towards it. I was thinking that I know why things are put in bins. *Behave yourself Baggy.* I stifled a smile as I was trying to avoid a rollocking as all I wanted to do was to become a good Firefighter in this great Service. The Station officer then piped up "Right then this morning we are going to slip and pitch the 135" (no surprises there then, and WE are going to slip and pitch it, not you Sir.) to the open window, (which was a large square hole in the wall 3 floors up, to the rear of a brick training tower) to teach you the 'Carry down." I quickly looked at the others who seemed ok with this. 'Eh? I thought the fire service stopped 'carrying' people down ladders and either escorted down live persons or they brought them down the internal staircase? It wasn't the thought of carrying anyone down BUT the thought of being carried down. "Right you lot, firstly three laps of the training building. GO."

The training building incorporated the training tower to the front and large BA fire training rooms for live firefighting scenarios to the rear; this was also where the large open window was situated for carry down drills. The whole structure was also known as the 'dolls-house' but did not resemble a dolls-house but a block of flats. We completed the three warm-up laps then lined up.

Four of us were ordered to slip and pitch the 135 to the open window as soon as the Instructor reversed the Dennis RS fire appliance from the end of the yard to where we were, which I thought that was rather considerate because I was half expecting four of us to leg it over to the appliance and fetch the ladder back. A volunteer was picked; not asked, but ordered to ascend the ladder and enter the hole and liaise with the Sub officer above who would harness him up. A large ringed eye hole protruded from above the aperture from the exterior wall. A safety line was passed through this loop-hole and clipped to the 'victim' to be carried down, the other end would be controlled by the Instructor so if the victim started to slip, they would not fall but be would be caught in a fall-arrest then lowered to the ground in a controlled descent.

A couple of carry downs were completed, and even though they tried to match weight and height you could still hear the ladder vibrating and rattling as the legs were wobbling with the extra weight on the backs of the rescuers. I was fortunate enough not to be picked for the victim, harness or no harness. I was next in line to demonstrate my carry down to the Instructors. I was told to make my way up inside the internal staircase to the third floor. My victim was all harnessed up and grinning at me, I gave him the *'you're not down yet mate'* look. He was taller than me, but then, who isn't! I was given the instruction method and then bent down to place my mate in a 'Fireman's lift' once I heaved him onto my shoulders the Sub officer made sure the harness was free as I turned round to step out onto the top of the ladder, lots of grinning faces looked up at us. The Sub officer gave me one more piece of advice "Watch his legs don't get caught as you swing out because he's such a long thing." I slowly stepped out and got myself and my extra weight comfortable at the head of the ladder and looked across at the Sub. He had the line in his hands and gave me the nod to descend. I started to descend slowly and got into a good pace; the ladder started making sounds as it did with the rest of the recruits; through my straining legs. I felt quite comfortable with the carry down, I wasn't sure if my mate was though. As long as you positioned the person right and locked them in, it was ok. We made it safely to the bottom. That's when I undid all my good work. We were told that when we stepped off the bottom of the ladder we were to turn away from the face of the ladder with one hand up to protect the head and face of the victim so that we did not injure him or her when turning away from the ladder. I carried this guy on my on my left shoulder so that his head was over my right shoulder, so my right hand should have gone up to protect his head and face. As I stepped away from the ladder I was so pleased with my descent that I nearly forgot to protect him as required. I quickly remembered the drill before I stepped away, but in my confusion, I put my left hand up whilst steadily turning away from the ladder. I turned to look at the other Sub, whilst smugly pleased with my rescue but the Sub looked at me with a confused and worrying look. Oh No what have I done, has the weight on my back passed out? Is he still alive? The Sub spoke "Baglow? Why are you protecting his arse?

I looked up to my right to see his head, and then looked to my left to see my hand in front of his backside, Ah. The Instructor looked at me whilst he nodded his head, grinning "Worried about you mate, worried about you!" he quipped. I could do nothing but laugh. I nearly forgot the drill then thought I'd better stick my protecting hand up, only to be the wrong one in the panic, typical.

During the carry-down drills we were dragged away (not literally) one-by-one into one of the training rooms to be tested on the Phonetic alphabet. For those who are not familiar with this system; it is used to identify the correct lettering of the alphabet in confirmation with a word for when using radio communication to banish confusion, so, for example, the letter **A** would be *'Alpha'*, **B**- *'Bravo'* and **C**- *'Charlie'* and so on. It is used widely within the military and emergency services fraternity.

So, I was up next. I had done a lot of brushing up on the phonetic alphabet, I knew it from a young age, so I just fine-tuned it. The instructor, a Sub O, fixed me with a steady gaze with a smirk on his face. "Baglow, Know the phonetic alphabet mate?" I returned the gaze blankly to the Sub O giving him no indication if I really knew it or not. The duel was on! "Yes Sub, I guess I'm ok with it." I said with a little fake uncertainly. The Sub looked on as he comfortably slumped in his seat. "Oh right, ok then what the phonetic wording for 'E'? I looked up to the ceiling, thinking. (I knew it really) "Um, Oh hang on, oh is it ECHO?" The Sub confirmed this as the correct answer. "Right, quicker, what about 'Y'?" I replied quicker as requested without the messing about. "Yankee, Sub." He continued "Z?" Again I was on it "Zulu." He now had an annoyed expression on his face as I'm sure he wanted to catch me out, or secretly wanted me to mess up. It was written all over his face. The Sub now thought that this was pretty easy for this cocky individual stood before him and so he upped the ante. "Baglow, spell your Christian and Sir Names using the phonetic alphabet without wavering throughout, see how you get on - GO." He gave me the look suggesting -*no way are you going to get this lot out at speed*.

I went for it at breakneck speed "Alpha, November, Tango, Hotel, Oscar, November, Yankee" then straight onto my Sir name. "Bravo, Alpha, Golf, Lima, Oscar, Whiskey."

The Sub sat up. "Right, ok, very good, now sod off." That was it! I was going to ask if that was a pass but thought I'd probably be pushing my luck.

After repeated drills and further introduction to new equipment and the ways of how the fire service do things, we were at the end of our recruits training. I had passed the recruits examination and assessment and went on to complete and pass the Breathing apparatus (BA) phase-one course. This meant I could be allocated as a Breathing Apparatus Entry Control Officer, or BACO, at a BA incident. A BACO wears a chequered black and yellow tabard near the point of entry of where the firefighters wearing BA would enter a building.

The wearers would normally enter in pairs but sometimes larger teams were required for search and rescue situations in very spacious areas, such as halls and warehouses. The duty of the BACO was to make sure the BA wearer was safely kitted out and had nothing out of place which could endanger him or the wearer's BA partner. The BACO collected their tallies, which were tabs with details written upon them that the wearer had filled in prior to attendance in chinagraph pencil; such as Name, the wearer's Brigade number, how much air they have in their BA cylinders on their back and time of entry. The BACO gives them the all clear to enter the building after confirming the crew's brief from the OIC; then calculate the time the crew should withdraw from the building; it should be in plenty of time before they have a total depletion of air. A 'low-air' warning whistle which is part of the set could be heard on the start-up as the air rushes past the whistle inlet then into the breathing system. If the air ran too low the warning whistle will sound to indicate that the wearer should be out of the building. The margin of approximately fourteen minutes is what the firefighter may have left to get out to fresh air safely. However, this could be reduced if the wearer had been physically exerting his or herself. The BA wearer, however, should NEVER wait for the whistle to sound before he or she starts to withdraw. Good BA wearers should always check their air gauges calculating how long it took them to get to the point at where they are and how long and how much air it would take them to get back out.

They should be out of the building WELL BEFORE the time of whistle. If that team is late out and/or radio contact is lost, then the BACO would implement a safety plan by sending in an emergency team to find them, then informing fire control. Every BA wearer had a 'distress signal unit' (DSU) attached to their BA set. This is in place in case a wearer found him or herself in trouble whether lost or injured. The wearer presses a button on the unit and this would emit a large warbling shrill which enable other wearers to hear it and to go toward the sound to give immediate aid to their colleagues. If the wearer was unconscious, so that he or she could not physically press the alert button then the unit would detect no movement in a short period of time and automatically send the distress signal. If the wearer was with another firefighter, but the distressed wearer could not be reached by their partner, then he or she could operate THEIR own DSU to attract attention for the troubled wearer.

So, I was now trained as a BACO, after the phase-one course I could actually wear BA **after** the initial fire had been extinguished by qualified BA wearers. I could then enter the building with a qualified Firefighter to learn the science of ventilation by opening certain doors and windows to achieve the desired effect of smoke evacuation without creating air entry into the affected area as to re-kindle the fire again, especially if crews were still turning over fire debris and dampening down.

In order to become a qualified wearer I had to attend and pass a BA 'phase-two' course, which included a couple of 'live' fire wears. This was to be a very exciting challenge.

Between normal drill sessions, fire calls and courses, the BNEC team continued to practice to strive for any improvement and honing of skills.

BREATHING APPARATUS TRAINING

T he BA courses that were held at Exeter, adjacent Fire Control and Headquarters, were brilliant, hard work, hot and sweaty, but excellent all the same. We were, firstly, introduced to the 'Spiromatic' breathing apparatus set and told about the safety margins, air capacity, how to clean, test and maintain and obviously wear the set. We then donned the apparatus; we placed the cumbersome cylinder on our backs tightened the straps, donned the facemask and took that first breath in order to breathe positive pressure air as opposed to normal ambient air. The facemask was slightly claustrophobic at first; accompanied by the slight rubber smell from the mask itself, but we got used to it. After familiarising with the facemask we were then instructed to push the Brigade Passenger Carrying Vehicle (PCV) around the complex which enabled us to breathe harder and appreciate the set, to grow confident with it. In the afternoon, the sets were washed, serviced then hung up, a lecture was then delivered by the training staff followed by a search exercise with a neckerchief around our heads masking the eyes in order to lose our sense of vision so that we had to feel our way around the BA chamber. We used the 'BA Shuffle' a technique when searching; this choreographed search technique allowed us to search in darkness without sustaining injuries. The 'BA shuffle' was used in such a way as all the weight was on your back foot, your front foot sweeping from side to side searching for holes in the floor, stairs, casualties, and weight testing the floor, your left or right hand (depending what side your search route you were on.) against the wall using the back of the hand to sweep up and down to feel for openings, door handles, windows etc. and to generally keep in contact with the wall to find your way out again, the other hand (back of the hand facing forwards) sweeping in front of you, vertical movements (we used to say sweep from nose to knackers.) to feel what's ahead such as walls, furniture, wires, debris etc. the reason why we didn't use the palm of the hand was because we would feel more sensitivity from the heat from fire through the doors that we were about to enter to check if it was hot or cold and the main reason is live electrics, if we felt palm first and touched a hanging live wire the hand would spasm and grip the wire plugging us permanently into the national grid! The back of the hand physically could not bend around a wire to grip it, so if a live wire was touched the hand immediately was thrown away from the source. Searching like this looked weird when watching others, likening to a culturistic tribal dance. But it was and still is deadly serious and could save our lives.

The next day the sets were back on. This time we had the facemasks blanked out with opaque mask stickers and we searched again, but with the weight of the cylinder and imposing mask attached to us.

Searching with blanking masks was actually worse than carrying out a search in smoke, at least with smoke there may be some air movement where we could get a slight break through it enough to work out a window with the light shining through, or a door's location, unless we were in absolutely thick black smoke. Before the second exercise the opaque stickers came off, we then searched in 'cosmetic' smoke, similar to 'dry ice' that was generated by a smoke machine, filling the chamber with masking 'smoke'. Throughout the remainder of the week we learned about self-rescue by removing our cylinders (but not masks) and squeezed ourselves through a small gap. One by one we crawled up onto a platform which on it was perched a large piece of hardboard with a square hole cut out of the middle of it, same size as two A4-sized sheets of paper. We were told that we should take our helmets off and offer it up to the gap and beyond, if our fire helmet could fit through a gap then so could we. And we did; then on the other side we put our cylinders back on. That was the self-rescue procedure in case we became trapped in rubble and such like. Another drill was to set off our Distress Signal Units (DSU's); when activated these devices were very noisy. DSU's were blue or grey electronic box-like devices which were attached to the left shoulder strap of the BA set. If a wearer experienced difficulty, was lost or injured.

In the training room we were told to sit on the floor in the darkened room, the instructors would tell us to activate our alarms and sit still as to 'conserve air' and await rescue and not to panic. The instructor would then walk out and close the door. Sat in that room having about twenty DSU's bashing the eardrums was not pleasant. I thought *wow this could be for real.*

At the time there was obviously no panic, but if trapped and conscious in a real situation then I think the adrenalin would start to kick in; and they do say adrenaline is brown! After a while of 'conserving air' the door was opened allowing in some light and we were told to stand up and collect out tallies to put an end to the endless racquet. The next day we had to clamber through a long concrete tunnel, which we could just get through crawling on our front and pulling ourselves forwards with our elbows and occasionally banging our facemask into the soles of the firefighter's boots in front. This exercise was practice in the use of High-expansion foam (HI-EX), which was used to extinguish fires in large areas such as ships holds, large warehouses and basements for example. This foam when pumped into an area in which it expanded vastly and filled an entire room from floor to ceiling. The use of HI-EX foam has now ceased as it was deemed environmentally unfriendly and expensive. Today crews now use compressed air foam system (CAFS) which pumps mixed foam compound and water through hose-reels to create jets of foam. I actually found the Hi-EX foam more disorientating than smoke as you lost your sense of hearing as well of your sight as the foam crackled into your ear canals. All you could hear after that were very distant muffled sounds. You had to shout even louder than normal through your mask to be heard (just about.) The foam was disorientating and claustrophobic. A BA instructor once set off an old DSU and placed the very noisy device into a bucket of HI-EX foam for demonstration purposes, once in, we could hardly hear it. Sadists designed this stuff! Anyway, Halfway up the tunnel we entered the foam, the foam entered the ears and crackled away- then nothing, no sounds of anyone breathing through their mask exhalation valves, no sounds of boots kicking at the tunnel to get through it, and a different way of feeling about us. After we dragged ourselves further up the tunnel we carried out a forward sweep with our arms, I couldn't feel the boots of the guy in front but I did feel a slight drop in floor level, the guy in front might have pointed out this hazard but I would not have been able to hear him. "STEP AHEAD" I shouted loudly to the firefighter behind me but that most probably had fallen on deaf ears, literally. The step down was about 30 Centremetres, on feeling around I felt the edge of the tunnel, and I climbed out, stood up slowly, felt a wall to my left and moved up and waited whilst the remainder filed out of the tunnel. We were now stood up in one of the rooms in the search chamber, now full of HI-EX foam. Nudging, poking, grabbing the others had now become the main course of communication unless we copped onto some words that were said. The brief to all of us was to search the room for any casualties and find our way to the far door to exit the room. Me and my BA partner found no casualties but did find the door (eventually) and headed outside with all foam bubbles blowing off our sets and fire kit in the light breeze. Others that followed us out looked equally funny.

"I'm glad that bloody things over with!" my mate shouted; he had a look suggesting that he didn't want to go through that again. I never saw ANY casualties lined up on the ground when we came out. The other teams found nothing. What were we playing at? Had we searched correctly even though the foam tried to throw us? We'll all probably get a ticking off for this one.

But nothing was said. Just praise for the hard work and effort put in. that was it. Hasten to say that we were then told that there were NO casualties in the room, fibbers.

The last day involved a big search and rescue exercise in the smoke chambers at a rapid pace. The instructors were now full on "Come on team one get your arses over hear, stop tossing about, its Persons reported. MOVE YOURSELVES." Team one got their brief and were in, as did team two, me and my mate were team four and waiting to go in. Team three were briefed and went in. We moved up to the instructor which is stood just to the side of the doorway that we are about to enter. "Right listen in" he snapped. And with a bit of ironic comedy proceeded to give us our brief "You have been called to 110 Clitoris Street................and you'll never find it! Ha ha." Very good! He continued "Four persons reported. I want you to go in on a left-hand search, ground floor search and rescue. REPEAT." I repeated the brief. "Right start up and go through BACO" We booked in with the BACO and rushed in. One minute into the search in a room to our left my mate felt an arm in the corner of the room; he felt a little more of the casualty which was now confirmed to be a small child (dummy, not real). "CASUALTY" he shouted; I radioed BACO to inform him of our find and as we headed out of the room we carried out a quick sweep to find no more persons. We bumped into team two on their way out "You got a casualty?" They asked us. "Yeah mate a child. We still need to search the ground floor." I said. "We've found a child but no more on our search so we are now withdrawing, we can take yours out if you like so you can continue" this was all discussed in a matter of seconds and low down near floor level as for the casualties would receive fresher air (as smoke rises). My BA partner handed ours over and we continued on our Left-hand search. In another room I felt a soft mass with my boot under a table, "REST" I shouted to my mate (meaning stop/wait in brigade parlance) I bent down and felt a leg and arm. "CASUALTY" I shouted, I radioed back the finding to the BACO and we grabbed the heavy adult dummy, after taking a gauge reading, of the amount of air left in our sets, we then withdrew with our casualty. A few 'casualties' were lined up outside. The exercise in that short space of time was very demanding in BA and disorientating. It was hot and sweaty and that was even without the presence of fire.

Heat and humidity training at the BA annexe was.....well, something else. The building that we had to enter was obviously very hot and extremely humid. The instructors ordered us to don full fire kit and BA, enter the building and carry out a range of exercises in this unforgiving heat for a time until you were on verge of passing-out, or at least it felt like it. Some forgot their names, others, including myself, became confused in answering questions and other just staggered out of the heat and felt nauseous or vomited after coming out. This training was to ascertain whether you could handle at least some heat 'punishment' as so you could deal with compartmental fires for real.

A month's time we would be attending the Service training centre in Plymouth to participate in 'Hot (real) Fire training', where we would be dragging large 70mm diameter hoses of 75 feet in length filled with water acting like a tube of heavy cement; knocking the fire back, producing steam and rescuing casualties.

Today the fire service has a training complex at Exeter International Airport which is home to a large 'House' "The VILLA" which the instructors may 'torch' time and time again for realistic search and rescue scenarios. Metal shipping containers adapted to entrain or occlude air in various fire behavioural situations form 'Attack pods' which are a great insight for recruits to see how fires behave and how hot it can get inside a structure. Other BA courses such as a Ships maritime course are offered. This is a very hot oily course as the 'ship', a metal structure of many layers (decks), is fired up to produce great plumes of black smoke. Because a ship is mainly metal, inside the ship the walls will retain the heat making it hotter than usual. Jets could be trained on the wall outside to act as a cooling effect, known as boundary cooling. I have been inside 'the ship' when it is on fire and I have never found boundary cooling that effective. The maritime course, even though very serious, was great fun. We learned how to don and pack lifejackets, stepping off diving boards into swimming pools in full fire-kit, scrambling aboard life rafts and bailing out the excess water and learning about ships stability during and after we poured water in. The whole 'stepping off diving boards' business was practiced on this course in case we had to evacuate a ship urgently; we would step off the side planting ourselves into the sea in the correct form as not to injure ourselves on impact.

Locally we had several exercises with our local Lifeboat crew who do an extraordinary job. We would gather on a weekend or a weekday evening and use the services of the local Lundy Island supply ship, incorporating the services of both the town's Inshore Lifeboat (ILB)and the All-weather Lifeboat (ALB) and sometimes the R.A.F. Search and rescue helicopter which would fly personnel and kit out to the 'stricken' vessel.. The supply vessel would be about a mile out in the Bristol Channel reporting to have a 'fire' on board accompanied with 'casualties' who were a great group of volunteers who would spend time in gruesome make-up with lacerations, burns, compound fractures and the likes.

Some of the fire crew were winched to the vessel whilst others used the services of the lifeboats to convey out to ship. Others would remain on the pier awaiting the eventual arrival of the ship that was now 'safe' to bring alongside. We then all tended to the casualties still on the vessel. The ALB also use their on-board firefighting capabilities on the exercise. The lifeboat crews then assisted us in casualty assessment along with the ambulance crews at scene. All communications were passed via the local coastguard crew that were summoned to the scene and rapidly attended and managed all communications swiftly.

We have also worked alongside the Coastguard teams on certain jobs before; and as with the lifeboat crews, they too do an outstanding job swiftly and effectively and all as volunteers. I had always enjoyed inter-service exercises. We can learn so much from such exercises as they can be out of our usual range of expertise; but a temporary amalgamation of all the services create a blend in that you get a sense of combined achievement that brings us together for one important aim – to rescue and save life.

BNEC – MANCHESTER

We arrived in Manchester on the Friday afternoon. Station officer Roy Hale accompanied us this time along with Station officer Golding. We also had two team members in reserve from the station with us, so one of them could support us and the other for the North Tawton team if required. We eventually found our hotel; as on the motorway in the Brigade's PCV Mike was sat in the front passenger seat with the window down; creating an air rush similar to a wind tunnel. Because of the brightness of the sun Mike done the obvious thing by lowering the sun visor, only to be attacked by a volley of paperwork which introduced itself to his face then proceeded to fly out of the window, this paperwork was our instructional documents that indicated the location and directions to our hotel and directions to Thompson street fire station where the BNEC event was being held, the paperwork now made new home across the tarmac of the motorway, there was no case sensitive documents at all. I was still drying my eyes by the time we did eventually check into our hotel in the city. We had a good look round, had a bite to eat then prepared for the night out. It was to be a sedate night out (as we thought); just a few beers and a chat about the on-coming events of the BNEC the next day. After we had visited several pubs we followed Terry and Mick into a niteclub. There was no evidence of a thriving queue of revellers who were just dying to get in there, nothing, anyway, we thought they may have been onto something as we eyed up the many posters enticing us to a great night within its four walls. The place looked very plush. We piled in only to be met with Terry making a very abrupt 'u' turn followed by Mick pushing past the rest of us who looked on in confusion. They were mumbling something like "SOD THAT I'm not paying sixteen pounds to get into a niteclub!" Who'd have blamed them? The rest of us agreed on hearing his statement and followed him out of the foyer very quickly. The niteclub down the road was slightly cheaper. I, for one, had to slow down on my drinking as I wouldn't be up in the morning, even though Jim had tempted us to take his charcoal tablets prior to befriending the alcohol. The club had large alcoves and women dancing within them. It looked very impressive, a few more 'half-pints' and an attempt at dancing followed by a slow walk back to the hotel. A few of the others remained out a bit longer. The boss was sharing a room with Ben, Terry with Jim and myself and Mick shared a room. There was a bit of chatting before one or the other dropped off to sleep, the brain was doused in too much alcohol to think about the BNEC event.

A set of repetitive knocks on the hotel door alerted us. BANG BANG BANG. I woke with a start Mick was now awake too. I then shouted out. "Hello?"

"Baggy, hurry up mate get changed and tell Mick too. We've only got an hour to get to the Fire station for registration, open the door." God it didn't feel like we had much sleep.

The room was still dark due to the ultra-thick curtain drapes. As we both began to spring out of our beds; Mick suddenly stopped the urgency.

"Hang on a minute bags, it's Jim, he's having a laugh, he's having us on." Jim was still at the door. "Come on boys, you don't want to be late." Mick fumbled for his wristwatch. "Don't open the door Mick he might have a fire extinguisher aimed at us!" I joked. Mick switched the light on and tried to focus on his watch "Bastard. It's only 3 o'clock in the bloody morning he's just got back from being on the lash." I glanced at my watch; and for no reason other for backing up my confused state of a mind I walked over to the window and pulled back a curtain to confirm that it actually was the early hours. Darkness over the rooftops of the city. "Sod off, it's three in the morning!" I shouted. Quietness returned to the other side of the hotel door once again apart from the odd chuckling floating up the corridor.

The morning of 7th of August 1998, we were up showered, dressed and just managed to get some breakfast down before sorting things out back at the rooms. Station officer Hale summoned the team into his room for a pre-event chat. Then we were off to Thompson Street Fire station (with replacement directions). It was another nice day. We, at times throughout the day, bumped into and chatted to the boys from North Tawton. As would be expected with a National event there was a large presence of numerous Fire-rescue teams in attendance. The first scenario was scheduled for 9am. We were due into the arena at 2pm. We had plenty of time to look round the various stalls and stands; we saw how the teams in the arena were getting on and absorbed some of their techniques of working. Unlike our small regional BNEC event where we had one scenario at a time, in the nationals they had four fenced off areas where four scenarios were at work simultaneously. A team had attended from South Africa too. We kitted up and entered the arena around 2pm. The scenario was a car on all fours (nice one Thank you) with one person trapped in the passenger seat. Myself and Terry both stabilised the car to good effect as expected with our on-going training, then on Sub officer Williams's orders we managed the glass by winding down windows, taking out the windscreen glass in one piece if we could do so, breaking both quarter-light glass with a spring-loaded centre punch; then cleared the glass away. We then both got to work removing the rubber door seals and plastic interior parts (due to the cutters preferring metal to cut through rather than trying to chew through rubber and plastic.) I covered both the medics and the casualty with a disposable transparent salvage sheet. It was loosely draped over them to protect them from further breakage of glass or metal fragments.

Mick had placed an oxygen mask on the victim. Ben was scouring the scene supervising and advising on a planned extrication method. *Roof flap back or full roof removal?* Ben approached me and Terry "We'll go for a roof flap boys ok?" I grabbed the cutters whilst Terry re-checked the stabilisation. For the roof flap back the roof is creased between the 'B' and 'C' posts, Relief cuts at the edges of the crease would have been cut prior to the crease being made. With the four 'A' and 'B' posts severed, and the windscreen cut lowdown or removed completely, the roof is then folded back along the crease thus flapping it back over the rear of the car. This was an excellent tactical decision for an extrication method as this offered space creation to the front seat occupants and afforded more time.

Usually we would normally go for a complete roof removal if there were persons trapped in the rear seats rather than look at carrying out roof flap forward method. If a full longboard removal were required then a full roof removal would be utilised for that scenario also.

The cutting tool was regimentally rotated between the post cutting between Terry and myself. The casualty was, again, released within the twenty minutes. Minor aspects were critiqued on the debrief such as moving tools right away from the vehicle when not in use as not to create a trip hazard and some medical checks were revised, but all in all very good. We all felt good about the evolution as we all put the hard work in as always. The other Devon lads looked like they were doing well when we sauntered over to watch them. A fire and rescue team from Newcastle won the challenge that day, but we all felt like winners, it was a great day and an epic experience. We all looked forward to another night out on the town after a meal in one of the plush local restaurants joined by the North Tawton team.

As we left the hotel for another night out; there were two fire engines outside the main entrance with their blue lights flashing and several firefighters walking into the hotel lobby. We caught up with some of the North Tawton lads that were looking on outside. "What's going on?" Ben asked them with obvious interest. The lad, still watching the commotion said "oh, they've got persons shut in the hotel's lift." We thought no more of it and headed off for a good night out. We scoffed ourselves silly and leaned back in our chairs reflecting on our fill when the OIC from North Tawton team walked over to our table "Club early for a dance and drink lads?" We all looked at him and Phil Golding pointed to our bloated abdomens of gluttony "Not likely. We'll need an hour for this lot to settle!" Their OIC then nodded and went to catch up with his blokes "Righto lads, I'll see you later." We visited several trendy establishments of refreshment and finally on the way back to the hotel we passed a very classy looking pub, very suave place, we all thought that we'd have some of that whilst attempting to act sober as not to put ourselves under a total intoxicated suspicion of the clientele. We were about to enter when the door supervisors turned Ben, me and Mick away as we were wearing jeans.

This establishment only entertained clientele who wore finely cut cotton suits and the likes (Joke) but 'smart' attire only. Fair enough, so we three walked away only to turn back to see the other two teasingly looking at us and walking into this place as their attire fit their description satisfactorily. They turned and came back out and teased that they wasn't going to go in without us and we should actually return to the hotel for more drinking.

We enquired to the hotel staff about the Fire Brigade's attendance earlier in the evening. They had the pleasure of telling us that six people were released from the lift and those six people were Firemen! They'd been taking part in the competition that day, returned to the hotel only to become shut in the lift, awkward. We didn't find out what team it was.

We had just started our long haul up the main staircase to our rooms when I spotted our two 'reservists' sat at the hotel's bar. We joined them for a couple more night-caps then plodded off up the stairs and left the two to continue sinking the beverages. I tried to nod off over the sounds of catering skips in the hotel's alley that clashed about and the melee of people still celebrating Manchester City's win over Man. United. We hadn't had as many spectators as they had at the soccer match that day, but the many spectators that we did have coupled with the atmosphere were second to none. In the morning we all joined up for breakfast, or at least what we could manage, as we walked down the stairs I looked over to the bar and to my disbelief our two team reservists were STILL sat at the bar, Obviously inebriated. That was some session, Luckily they wanted room to spread out and sleep on the journey home so decided to travel back in the less cramped North Tawton's van. Later when we both stopped for fuel we saw the both of them slouching on the side step of the PSV holding their heads.

"The drill will be to Slip and pitch the 1.3.5. to the third floor of the drill tower, One line of 45mm hose consisting of 2 lengths to be carried aloft and got to work at the head of the ladder. Do you understand the drill?" Leading firefighter McGovern addressed his two crews that were stood smartly to attention in front of him. One crew was to work the ladder the other to set out the hose and climb aloft in readiness for firefighting. We all shouted simultaneously our acknowledgement. "Good- CREWS AS DETAILED – GET TO WORK."

The crews split up and swung into action utilising the whole of the drill yard. The ladder was pitched against the third floor sill, two lengths of hose were laid out, the first length that terminated at the branch, placed over the 'branch-mans' shoulder and he rapidly ascended the ladder. At the top just below the sill he took a 'leg-lock' (placing his leg through two rounds (rungs) and locked his foot behind the lower round. He then placed the branch either under his arm or over his shoulder, and while shouting down instructions for water, his mate beneath him was creating a large bight in the hose and securing it to the ladder with a 'hose becket'. The bight is created as for when the firefighter advances into the building he will not have to heave lots of heavy water-filled hose all the way up from the drill ground.

The bight had created enough slack to easily make an advance without too much effort. "WATER ON - NUMBER ONE DELIVERY - WORKING FROM THE HEAD OF THE LADDER - 3 BAR PRESSURE." The instruction was shouted to the runner on the ground, the firefighter's instructions were repeated back to him in confirmation and the message then relayed to the pump operator who steadily opened the delivery and increased the throttle revolutions to obtain enough pressure to assure the water reached the branch-man but steadily enough as not to knock the hose from his grip; or worse; the branchman off the ladder himself. The branchman may ask for an increase or decrease in pressure as he so wishes. "KNOCK OFF - MAKE UP." Leading firefighter McGovern shouted for all fire-fighting operations to cease and the gear to be made-up (put away.) The drill just carried out was a basic warm-up drill. This particular drill was known as a 'combination drill' as it consisted of ladder and hose work together, sometimes incorporated BA as well.

We may sometimes just carry out pump/hose drills, ladders, combination, BA, Chemical protection suits and RTC drills. These could also be performed off-station, in or on other buildings as much as risk assessment prevails. They don't always have to be practical sessions; we could have lectures, and topography sessions (area knowledge such as locations of roads, locations of hydrants etc.) Tests will have to be carried out such as vehicle checks, ladder inspections and pump tests such as pressure, output and vacuum tests. We always took our drills seriously but we did have light-hearted moments. Such an occasion was when we were partaking in some combination drills under the scrutinising eyes of Station officer Golding and another officer, an Assistant Divisional Officer (ADO) as it was my probationary tests back in 1997. Last day as a probie, if I passed.

The interview went well, kit familiarisation went well, Question & Answer session went well also the unnerving drills went well, so overall a good night.

I was called into the office where the ADO, Sub officer Derrin and Station officer Golding sat at the ready. Terry had a slight crease on his face as I walked in and looked straight at him, so I thought it might be good news. The ADO looked up "Take a seat. How do you think it went this evening FF....ah........................Baglow?" He snapped the Surname out at the last second. I thought that's great that is, he can't even remember my name. In short of replying 'well sir my night seems to be going better than yours' I rid that one from my mind very quickly and replaced it with "I would say it has gone very well Sir. I think that I have demonstrated most tasks to the best of my ability, thankyou Sir." The ADO took a deep breath, OH NO, WHAT? I thought; but waited patiently. "I think you have performed very well indeed firefighter Baglow and I am pleased to inform you that you have completed your probationary period successfully. Well done." Everyone shook hands all around the room whilst I could hear drills still continuing outside under the command, this time, of leading firefighter Stone.

I walked out into the drill yard beaming. Stoney looked over at me, "Well done Bags." the others turned round and offered their congratulations accompanied with a couple of over-zealous back-slaps. "Get some fire kit on bags, were just going through the Hughes ejector pump, we're going to lift from open water." Stoney then turned back to the others "Right lads, short extension ladder, salvage sheet, lines and fill the dam up. Someone fetch the ejector pump and hose." I walked over to the muster bay and start donning my kit. Eh? Its 8.50pm, we're meant to knock off drills at 9 pm and usually start to make the kit up, not get it out. I thought no more about it and walked back into the drill yard. The dam had been made and water from the hydrant via the pump was being trained into the dam to fill it up. The Hughes ejector pump (HEP) is a primitive but effective piece of hydraulic apparatus.

Now for the basic science bit on hydraulics within the job - We **lift** water in the fire service, via 100mm hard suction hose, wire-supported non-collapsible hose. We had four lengths to each pump. The hose would screw together by threaded joins then tightened with suction wrenches, as not to entrain air through the joins and lose vacuum. With a strainer at the end we would place the sections of hose into open water source such as a lake pond, sea etc. the air is expelled from the hose via the pump, this creates a vacuum in the hose and water is forced from its source and in turn lifted up into the pump, which in turn is pumped to the firefighting hoses through the deliveries, voila! People have a misconception that fire engines suck water. A fire engine doesn't suck water up into its pump. It would need an extremely powerful massive engine to suck water up four sections (or more) of 100mm hose into the pump.

The other form of lifting water is with the HEP, this is a metal 3-way port connection which is shaped like the letter 'T' it is formulated precisely. Basically water is fired at high pressure into it at one end and across the 'T' through to the other side horizontally. Whilst water is traversing this apparatus at high pressure a vacuum is created in the hard suction hose, hanging below placed in water vertically, and the water is forced up the suction hose (lifted) which also gets fired out the HEP into a firefighting hose, but; with a constant supply of water. The HEP can be suspended on a ladder or by line. The whole process of lifting water with this method is called the 'Venturi effect.'

If we had just extinguished a fire in a building but it was still smoke logged, as long as it was clear of people or buildings opposite the affected property; then we could open a large window and fire a powerful spray jet out of the window. This high pressure creates a low pressure around it and you would observe all the smoke rapidly following the water out of the window, thus clearing the smoke. Again, the Venturi effect. Good eh? I have actually used this method of smoke extraction once; and it worked effectively. They actually just open windows and use positive pressure ventilation fans nowadays.

Anyway, I greatly digress. Back to the drill yard. The lads had now filled the dam and stretched a line from one edge to the other with the HEP set above the water ready to lift it. We got to work throwing a bit of water about whilst the Officers were milling about in the appliance bay having finished their discussion upstairs. Stoney then called for it to be knocked off but NOT make-up. Strange, I thought as time was knocking on and the dam still stood full of water. The Leading firefighter then asked for the HEP to be made up and put away but said nothing about making up the dam. He just kept chatting about vacuums and pressures while he kept glancing over at the officers chatting. I looked about at the few of the lads and they seemed unperturbed to the on-going drill at this time of night.

Normally they're chomping at the bit to get away from drill. One by one the officers started to leave, the Station officer stopped momentarily to talk to the Sub as a few of the lads approached me then backed off when they saw he was still talking. Then as I looked at the officers it dawned on me..... OH NO! End of probationary period, I passed, they've built a dam (which has nothing to do with the drill) and they're waiting for the officers to bugger off. OH NO, this is the sign of their celebratory efforts of the end of my probation and so for the 'dunking! They wouldn't do it whilst the officers were still about. I was ready to pick my moment to run. Two of the lads asked if they could go as its 9pm and had things to do, which was granted (two less to witness my embarrassment) I was just about to ask if I could go when I heard the goodbyes of the two Officers and the Sub traipsing back up to the office. GO! I made a run for it as I am chased on-mass. I legged it round the side of the station and saw the two lads 'that needed to get away' coming at me from the side.

I paced it up a bit and escaped them and ended up off station outside a row of houses, I was now thinking "Where you going to go from here Bags, in to town?" I sprinted back across the road into the station garden and tried to get round the back. As I tried to squeeze through the fencing I was momentarily trapped and then caught "come on Baggy, behave yourself mate." I was carried by 4 firefighters to the dam. "You shits, the boss is still about y'know?" SPLASH! I'm thrown into the water and popped back up to unleash my torrent of abuse at the laughing 'kids'. I was still laughing and spluttering as I went to change my kit over to dry fire kit. I had been an accomplice to many a dunking to other post-probies after that.

FIRST 'LIVE' B.A. WEAR – PERSON'S REPORTED

"FIRE - BOTH PUMPS AND THE BRONTO FROM BARNASTAPLE" (014) someone shouted exiting the watchroom with tip sheet in hand. The Bronto could be described to the layman as a glorified, but very sophisticated, cherry picker. The reader, if not familiar with Fire Brigade vehicles and equipment would see these large fire appliances with their hydraulic booms high up in the air overlooking a fire incident training water on the fire itself, or used in a high level rescue role or to elevate officers to get an overall picture of the incident from a 'birds-eye view'. The Bronto's have superseded the old Turntable ladder (TL) which were effectively sections of ladders that were automatically raised and extended which allowed the firefighter strapped in at the top of the leading section to utilise the water monitor in order to direct a high-pressured water jet into the heart of the fire. The TL that was stationed at Ilfracombe had the call sign 024, and took pride and place on station from the 1950s up until 1996 when it was transferred to Barnstaple thirteen miles away to take up position with other specialist vehicles there.

The address was shouted out and established that this was a building fire at the sea front area, persons reported. This meant that there were possibly people trapped inside the building either being succumbed by the thick toxic smoke or by fire itself. I was still only qualified as a BACO only and a 'ventilation' wearer. So I got myself in the middle seat on 021, donned my fire kit as fast as I could, discarded my shoes out of the window onto the station floor (where everyone's went) I put on my black and yellow tabard, grabbed my BA Entry control board and was ready to go. The engine was fired up. I looked across to see that 022 were quickly filling up and they're crew frantically getting their kit on having received the urgent nature of the incident. With blue lights on which flicked eclectic beams from the strobes and two-tone sirens sounding we both left the fire station in convoy. The sirens had a two-fold purpose of warning the traffic that we were coming, to make way, also to alert the person(s) trapped that help was on its way. We pulled up outside the property, which were flats above a shop. I briefly glanced up and saw that there was grey/black smoke issuing from a flat's first floor window which was situated above a flat roof of the shop below. Many people gathered to watch the drama unfold. My nerves started to kick in again as I set up the entry control board against the wall of the shop. The first BA team were rigged and by my side, a hosereel also laid out for them by our driver. Their brief from Sub O Derrin was to search and rescue any persons that they found and to 'knock out' any fire.

They handed in their tallies, repeated their brief and whilst I marked down their time of entry and calculated their 'due out' time. I awaited a second team to rig and approach entry control. I turned and recognised a local chap who stated that he had saw an elderly lady at the front first floor window. *Oh Shit*, I thought to myself and immediately relayed this information to the Sub.

"RIGHT COME ON, CONFIRMED PERSONS REPORTED!" He yelled across the fire ground to get more BA wearer's in. Then he radioed the BA crew that had already entered and told them what the situation was in hand then called for a 'make-up' due to the nature of the call. A make-up is when an OIC requests more pumps or specialist appliances. I lifted the entry board up to prepare to write in the details of the next team. Jim Stone approached me, lowered the board to the ground and pointed to our pump. "Leave that Bags, go and get a set (BA) on." I looked at him in a confused manner. "Eh? I'm only qualified as B......"

"I know" he quipped in reply, "Terry knows too but we need wearers now. We've got someone else to take over BACO, Give him the tabard and get a set on mate." I passed the tabard to the waiting firefighter and jumped into the back of 021. I urgently pulled the BA set from its seating and adjusted the cylinder onto my back, the facemask strap round my neck ready to don as soon as we were briefed. I fumbled with the harnesses and straps due to my trembling hands. Finally I stepped down from the pump and noticed that Jim had just adjusted his BA straps at the entry control. I concentrated in transferring my nervous energy into aggressive energy for strength stamina and endurance as this was going to be a rescue situation, my first one. The Sub jogged over to us and gave us the same brief as the first team. I could hear over the BACO's radio that the first team had found the fire and were initially involved in firefighting. "Right, start up. You got you're brief, in you go." Terry watched us start up the sets and check each other then entered the building. He knew all too well as regards to urgency on these shouts owing to the years' service that he had achieved of nearly thirty years at the time of writing. We could see part way up to the return of the stairs on the first floor until the smoke became thicker, then visibility was right down. We followed the hosereel that had been hauled in by the first team. We kept the tubing between our feet which took us straight to the flat involved, which made life easier. As we felt our way through the kitchen we saw the first BA crew firefighting a severe fire in the front bedroom. We felt a closed door to our left of where the fire was so we carried out door checks for any signs of fire behind the door. We cracked the door open slightly whilst we remained in thick smoke, most of the smoke had found its way under the door into the lounge once the fire took hold. We kept low and bumped into the side of a sofa as we edged forward. As we searched about we caught sight of movement in the intermittent smoke swirls. With my hands I felt an arm Jim's hand was on it too "We've got someone." his shout muffled through his mask. We discovered an elderly lady lying on the sofa. She was conscious and breathing. We unceremoniously gathered her up from the sofa and got her to the French window that faced the front of the building.

Jim radioed down to BACO to organise a crew to get a ladder to the first floor flat roof. It was still far too dangerous to take her back through the thick smoke and risk her near the still raging fire in the next room. I shut the lounge door and opened the glass doors and we ushered the woman out into fresh air of the summers evening. I looked at the woman to check that she was still ok, I noticed that she had cotton wool sticking out of her nose AND ears, probably a panic trigger to stop the ingress of smoke. A short extension ladder was placed against the side wall of the flats and rested on the edge of the flat roof. Sub O Derrin, himself, climbed up to escort the woman down the temporary escape to safety. She didn't require the old 'fireman's lift' and managed to slowly climb down the relatively short distance under the guidance of the Sub.

Myself and Jim then found our way back out into the hall and into the neighbouring bedroom to assist the first crew with the fire that was challenging them. They've worked the hosereel to good use with now only a small fire climbing up the wall in the corner of the room. The heat build-up was intense. If the reader can imagine standing quite close to a large bonfire on a hot summer's day, you will experience quite intense heat which uncomfortably tingles on your skin. Now put that fire in a bedroom, let it involve the room and its contents for five minutes and you would understand the notion of what its really like to work in an enclosed hot fire environment.

Me and Jim were tasked to check other nearby apartments within the building as the smoke had liberally spread throughout. We first returned outside, but didn't shut down our sets as we had plenty of air and only went to collect a sledgehammer in case we needed to force entry. We informed BACO of our intentions as so that he could mark it down in the comments section on the control board. We re-entered the smoke filled building and were informed over the radio that the fire was now extinguished and that the crew were turning over and damping down. We now had permission to open a few windows and doors in the vicinity to rid some of the thick smoke. We knocked on doors up and down the building, no answers. We had to check the flats in case someone had collapsed with a medical condition brought on by the smoke or the drama itself. We commenced breaking in using the sledgehammer revealing that the flats were a bit 'smitchy' with smoke but no sign of occupants. I could hear heavy footsteps coming up the stairs and saw, through the now thinning smoke, two firefighters who had come to take over the task from us. We handed over our sledgehammer, pointed out the area that we had already checked and informed BACO that the flats searched so far had no occupants within them and that we'd passed on our task to another crew and were now withdrawing from the building. Halfway down the stairs Jim turned to me and we 'hi-fived' each other. "Well done Bags.

Good job mate." He shouted. In a similar muffled voice I congratulated him also on a job well done.

I half expected to change our cylinders and return to the building to ventilate, as I would do in a flash seeing that my adrenaline was still at its peak. As we reported to entry control to collect our tallies I noticed other crews entering the premises to take on the task of ventilation and to damp down. We both removed our sets and placed them carefully on the ground at the BA cleaning area. But before we cleaned the sets and changed the near empty cylinders for full; we guzzled loads of bottled water to re-hydrate again, the remainder poured over our heads to cool ourselves down. The first team were now at entry control having just withdrawn from the building, they then joined us in BA cleaning, and they too looked hot, flushed and knackered. We all agreed that this fire was a good 'stop'. A 'stop' is usually defined as a radio message at the end of an incident or when no more back-up appliances are required. Every twenty minutes an 'informative' message is sent to control to inform them of ongoing progress. If this is a longer protracted incident the informative message can be sent every hour. If there are no injuries, no major fire spread, other buildings spared from fire, persons rescued etc. We then class that as a 'Good Stop.' Four pumps and several hours later, we left the scene and headed back to station for more cleaning. The first team mentioned that there was also a small fire in the kitchen that they quickly 'knocked out' on the way to the main fire in the bedroom. The rescued lady was fine and doing well.

RTC PRACTICE SESSIONS

The BNEC team were together once more for intense RTC sessions in the drill yard. We had frequent breaks as sometimes full on rescue work was difficult, hot, and you could become very sweaty and dehydrated through physical handling of the tools and casualties, especially as we were wearing full fire kit and rushing about in a methodical manner. I used to carry a face flannel or two either in my tunic pockets or under my fire helmet. On one particular occasion we had just finished a break. I removed my dark blue towelling flannels and placed one corner of each flannel up under the sides of my fire helmet leaving the remainder of the material hanging down over my ears like 'Deputy Dawg' it wasn't a photo opportunity at the time but after the laughing and pointing had died down we were about to commence with the drill when I realised my 'new ears' were still hanging there.

Terry looked into the CUEES rules and policies as regards to deflating of any crashed vehicle's tyres after we had blocked the vehicle under the sills. This method would guarantee a positive stable platform as the weight of the car would be taken up by the car body itself sat on the blocks rather than air still in the tyres bouncing the thing around especially if a block or wedge was dislodged. There was nothing in the ruling stating we could not carry out this deflation method. So we devised a technique for rapid deflation. The unscrewing of the dust-cap and offering something into the inflation valve pin to release the air was too fiddly and slow. We then experimented in knifing the tyres, so inserting a locked-knife's blade into the wall of the tyre; this method was messy as we wanted to let the air out to lower the vehicle in a controlled manner. Terry and I discussed deflating the front two tyres first, by using an arm signal to state that we were both ready followed by a 'GO' then the same with the rear two tyres. The knife technique still proved uncontrolled and one side of the vehicle lurched about followed by the other side. We definitely did not want a side-way movement, due to the casualty/s C-spine consideration, but a forward and backward motion was just about permissible, minimally. No movement would be Ideal, in an ideal world. But owing to difficult situations and working on the vehicle this was not always possible. We obviously needed a stable platform in preparedness for the medic to enter the car to assess and treat the casualty/s. By the next practice session Terry had acquired two wheel valve removers; these devices were basically 20cms of metal handle, an open round tube-like aperture at one end accompanied by a recessed-step next to it. To remove the valve we placed the step on the wheel's rim, after placing the aperture around the valve, and simply pulled the lever, in doing so this removed the valve from the tyre completely thus expelling the air and in turn deflating the tyre. Even though the hole that resulted was actually bigger than a knife incision the air flow was quite controlled.

We practiced with this method on several occasions; which were witnessed and approved by the Teams OIC. Terry and I spent several days during the week in the drill yard mastering our stabilisation skills by repeated chocking and blocking practice, utilising wedges and blocks of choice for different scenarios. We would stand next to each other a little way from the vehicle we were practising on, with a box of chocks and blocks each placed in front of us. On the shout "GO" and we would grab our respective boxes and proceed to stabilise the car starting at the front working back. We were very quick by now working like formula 1 mechanics when changing a wheel! We got the time down to twenty five seconds on stabilising a car which was on all four wheels. Terry was a great mentor on these sessions and passed on his knowledge from stabilisation to cutting and spreading work, he offered a constant commitment to the job as a whole, socially with the staff, and the team. His and Sub O Williams crews also returned their commitment to all aspects and that made everyone feel belonged and proud.

FIRST QUALIFIED BA WEAR

I t was a Tuesday evening, the crews had just finished a pump and ladder drill, known as a combination drill, and had made up all the kit and put the pumps back into the appliance bay. I felt quite proud of myself as a few days previous I just passed my BA course phase 2; which qualified me to wear BA at any incident as and when required. I had just hung my tunic on my peg and rolled down my fire leggings ready to step out of when the system went down. I pulled up my leggings again, grabbed the rest of my kit, heaved it all on and pulled myself up into 021. Sub O Derrin shouted through the clamber and chatter "021 and 022 – FIRE." He then jumped on board 021 as our OIC, whilst Sub O Williams climbed aboard 022 to command its crew. I was third man in the appliance seated in the middle (BA 4). If the first team of BA wearers were required then BA1 and BA2 were situated in the outside seats, they could get out first without scrambling past the other two. BA 3 would grab the entry control board and tabard and 4 would do the general fire-ground duties. If a second BA team was required they would be BA 1 and BA 2 off the second pump. If, however, there was no second pump for a while or the OIC wants as many BA crews as he could to achieve a rescue for instance then he would order the BACO and the runner to don their sets from the middle and pass the entry control board to the pump operator, who has to look after the hydraulic pump pressures, check the hydrant, keep an eye on the BA entry control and may have to render first aid to casualties. And as one pump operator so edgily put it "why not stick a broom up my arse and I'll sweep the floor 'an all!" As I was BA 4, the runner, I was thinking that it would be unlikely that I'd get a wear on this job. Terry turned to us in the back "Book us out will you. "Fire at the 'Olde Cyder Apple pub'. Chip range on fire." I knew this building well. It was a nice quaint public house on the edge of town. I was thinking about what I should be doing when we eventually arrive when Harry next to me acting as BA 2 nudged me. "Get a set on bags, you can go in mate." I looked at him questioningly. "It's your BA job though Harry." He sat back relaxed "Nah, go on mate, you might as well get the experience." I was now like a kid that's got all the sweets. "Right, ok. Ta mate."

I quickly donned a set knowing that we couldn't be far from the address. I glanced across to the far side of the pump to see who was riding the BA 1 position. In the partial darkness I saw someone's helmeted head down adjusting his set straps but I clocked it was a Leading firefighter identified by the one black bar around the fire helmet. I carried on rigging my set and glanced over once again to found I would be wearing with Jim Stone. We pulled up outside the property, no obvious smell of burning or smoke. The BACO ran over to the pavement and set up just outside the door. I stepped down from the pump and joined Jim at BA entry control. On my way I looked up to the first floor and saw a large teasing orange glow behind a large blackened window. My mouth felt extremely dry.

Sub O Derrin gleaned some information from possibly the owner or staff member then came over to us. "Right boys listen in. Chip range on fire in the first floor kitchen. Go through the rear door, up the stairs and go left at the top, the kitchen is ahead of you. Clear?" Jim, being Number 1, confirmed the brief and I acknowledged it. I started thinking '*chip pan range? Looking at that glow up there it looks as if it had taken hold and the whole kitchen's alight."* I heard Sub O Williams as he called for a Dry Powder (DP) extinguisher to be brought to us as this fire was involving hot oil, a class 'B' fire. Applying water onto it would only exacerbate the situation by causing a volatile reaction with the hot oil resulting in a severe conflagration within the kitchen. With the DP extinguisher in my hand, tallies in the BA board and air pressures checked I followed Jim in through the door and up the stairs. Half way up the stairs we encountered thick smoke devilishly swirling as it mixed with the air. We dropped to our knees and crawled along the hall. The smoke was less thick here and we could just make out a flickering glow up ahead through the door that was ajar. The radio crackled into life "BA team 1 from BA control, were sending in another team to back you up, over." I fumbled for the press-to-talk button of my radio which was attached to the strap of my set I lifted it to my facemask and shouted my acknowledgment. We wasted no time as we inched further into the thick smoke-logged passage. We cracked the door a little more and remained low as to see where the fire was and if there were any fire spread. Some curtains were involved in fire but mainly confined to the chip range. I pull the safety retaining pin on the DP and passed it to Jim who was in front of me; he then attacked the flaming range with a few well aimed intermittent blasts from the DP extinguisher. This knocked the fire completely out, now the air was filled with the acrid smoke and dry powder. The second team were now heading towards us from down the hallway I could hear their breathing and saw there DSU lights flashing. Not much for them to do now apart from checking the rest of the kitchen and venting. This was carried out to good effect. When the last smitches of smoke has cleared, the room remained quite hot, with the walls retaining all heat from the fire. There was a film of dry powder everywhere; like smoke, this stuff spreads and finds its way into every nook and cranny. I pulled down the rest of the, now molten, curtains and ventilated the immediate area and removed some of the burnt material to open air. Outside I mentioned that it looked as though the whole kitchen was alight initially as we turned up. Harry replied that is was because it was such a free burning bright fire within a wall of smoke that the smoke actually diffused the fire, spreading the glow across the room through the smoke that had the effect of looking larger than it actually was. The owners and staff had done the right thing on seeing that the fire was fully established, by trying to close the door of the room involved, evacuating the building and calling 999. This was my first 'qualified' BA job I had attended.

And it felt great. When we got back on station I took my BA set off the pump and walked over to the cleaning room. Sub O Derrin was walking towards me with a big grin on his face; he spoke and said "WELL DONE FIREFIGHTER."

BNEC - PLYMOUTH

S unday 27th September 1998. Back on the motorway again, this time back to Service training centre at Plymouth for the BNEC regionals in which we had once again applied for. We had trained hard for this. *Let's get through to the Nationals again, that would be great.* There were a few teams down at Plymouth this particular year including, again, the team from North Tawton. We watched the North Tawton boys extricate a casualty from a difficult 'car on all fours' scenario, then we went to check the equipment area to select a few extra tools. After that task; whilst out of the way being briefed, the organisers prepared our scenario. Whatever the scenario that had been set we decided on this particular scenario to immediately stabilise the vehicle using the tyre valve removers, and do a quick recce of the wider area around the vehicle to assure that no-one had been 'ejected from the vehicle or hit by it'. Up to now we had not witnessed this strategy by other crew's searching they're immediate area of operations. It could happen for real but the chances of seeing this carried out in the BNEC were very slim, although I had seen it in place on an exercise. It would look like we are conscious of what could happen as regards to other persons ejected or hit, not just the trapped victims, just being conscientious and extra vigilant. We were called into the arena. We all jogged in to see the scenario that faced us, car on all fours, two front seat occupants trapped. I quickly looked up toward the viewing galley, lots of people watching from other teams also our own families, I spotted my children Sasha and Craig with beaming smiles on their faces poking over the parapet. The families came to support us and make it a day out. We were blessed with fine weather once again. Jim and Mick took their medical kit to the front of the vehicle and talked to the one conscious casualty through the missing windscreen. Mick passed instruction to him to look straight ahead and not to move his head or nod and to acknowledge his questions he must just say yes or no. Jim had gone to ascertain the other casualty predicament, to check if he was unconscious or deceased. Ben was supervising our stabilisation; some blocks were working loose so, me and Terry desperately looked for some wedges to push gently home to squeeze the actual block stack tightly between the car body and the ground. We both started at the front and worked backward trying to work in unison, apart from scrambling for wedges in the chock/block box. The tyre-valve remover was put to good use.

We called out to the OIC and the medics when we were done and whilst one of the judges moved in to scrutinise the challenging stabilisation Terry and I started our little jog around the car for any missing or ejected persons. One of my family mentioned to me afterwards that a member of another team who was watching observed us running around the car looking for......well, nothing, and commented "What are those two doing? They're running around like headless chickens."

To be fair, I bet it did look a bit odd but, that quick search gained us points in doing so as the judges knew exactly what we were doing. Jim indicated to Ben what the situation was with the casualties. The passenger was deceased and not trapped, the driver was injured but no neck or back pain but had fractures to the lower legs but had feeling and sensation in hands and toes, so no nerve damage, he was trapped by the foot-pedals (de ja vous! - Prologue) and in need of extrication (what else on a BNEC day). Ben was now with us "Jim suggested the best way of extrication was probably a 'B'-post rip. We could remove the deceased casualty out of the side door. The judges had advised that Police and Ambulance were now on scene so that may free up Jim or Mick for you if needed ok?" I nodded "ok let's do it." Adrenaline was flowing, I grabbed more blocks and a couple of wedges and packed below the middle ('B') post, as Terry slickly connected the cutters and spreaders to the generator in readiness, we both then sorted the glass management and removed all rubber and plastic away to expose the metal that had to be cut and spread. The reason behind the 'B' post rip is that it affords access via space creation along the whole length of the car; when there is no need to remove the roof. On this occasion we wanted the ambulance crew to splint the fractured legs so it was best to have the victim flat as possible and brought out of the side. It was much better for crews too, as it afforded space that we wouldn't have if the 'B' post was in situ and just moved the door only. One bent pedal, the accelerator, was trapping the foot. One of the judges talked to Ben "The casualty now had pain relief." Ben passed this message on to Jim. We used an ad hoc technique to re-locate the offending accelerator pedal. We had used it several times on drills and it had worked affectively. Terry taught me this method and it was a neat technique. He removed a piece of rolled seatbelt out of this tunic and unfurled it. The long piece of webbing had a 3 inch slit lengthways at one end of the webbing, this was terminated at the end with a knot as so the slit didn't tear beyond the end. Terry ducked into the footwell and slipped the slit end over the pedal and assured that the casualty's foot would not be injured when we moved the pedal. Seeing that this was only the one disjointed pedal we'd rather this quick and effective method rather than resorting to the hacksaw blade again! We still did not have a pneumatic pedal cutter in Devon fire and rescue at the time. He then kept the tension on the webbing and got up from out of the footwell. "There you go Tone." he handed me the other end. I closed the door slightly and gradually pulled and wound the seatbelt tight around the framework of the door, I had wrapped the end of the seatbelt three times around the actual door frame itself. We then both grabbed the seatbelt and the door frame and with one controlled movement we opened up the door fully. This movement had just relocated the offending pedal to one side and in doing so freed the casualty's foot. This done, we quickly moved on to perform the remainder of the 'B' –Post rip.

I grabbed the cutters "ENERGISE GREEN" I shouted over to Mick, who was now at the generator, to indicate that I needed the hydraulic fluid running through the green hydraulic hose to operate the cutters, he repeated the request and moved the lever. I proceed to make a horizontal cut at the bottom of the 'A'-Post adjacent to the sill.

The rear unaffected door opened freely when Terry tried the handle. He then used the cutters and cut completely through the top of the 'B'-Post in one cut and immediately dropped down to make one horizontal cut to the rear of the bottom of the same post adjacent to the door sill but deliberately didn't cut it through completely. I picked up the spreaders. "ENERGISE ORANGE." Mick switched the lever over to the orange hose to operate the spreaders as I offered the closed jaw tips into the low partial horizontal cut that Terry had just made, I added a bit of weight to the tool and slowly opened the spreader jaws as terry was adding leverage to the 'B' post; slowly but surely the metal split along the sill, Tony joined me to add to the force of tool to assure it remained in situ without slipping. When the spreader jaws were fully open I closed the jaws and repositioned the tips to attempt another rip. The jaws again slowly opened to achieve a full rip of the lower 'B' post until the metalwork literally popped apart and ripped clear. "Neutralise tools" another request as Mick made safe both tools. He then jogged back over to the car to assist with pulling the rear door, the 'B'-Post and the front door (which was now only held on its hinges) we pulled the whole free side forward to the front wing; a line was then attached to the back door frame and the whole side pulled tight and secured to a towing eye or, as in this case, the front axle. We now had an impressive open space from where the doors originally were. Time was ticking away. I realise my thirst is getting worse. "Ok, stretcher is now at the door. Let's think about getting him out." Ben told the team. The casualty's legs splinted and pain relief administered by the imaginary ambulance crew we all mucked in and slowly eased the now un-trapped casualty to the stretcher. The whistle had not yet sounded so we must still be within the twenty minutes. The judge walked up to the team "Ok Fellas, well done. That's it. Go and get a drink." Another 20 minutes went by and the team learned both good and bad points from the de-briefing. After that all the teams were gathered in the large social room and bar area on the first floor of the training centre. Station officer Golding announced the results. This time he announced only one winner and that went to Ilfracombe! We had gone through to the National extrication challenge to be held in in Bonnie Scotland next year.

THE BIG 'CLIFFE'

Several times throughout the year our crews had attended shouts to a derelict hotel, The '*Cliffe Hydro hotel*'. This building was once a glamorous hotel with rooms overlooking the pretty harbour area from its high vantage point. It had been derelict for a number of years and we had numerous fire calls to this building, some large some small, some difficult to find the seat of the fire.

One Saturday afternoon we were called to 'smoke issuing'. Both 021 and 022 were required along with the Bronto 014 from Barnstaple station. We arrived and booked in attendance at the scene but saw no obvious signs of smoke. Our OIC Sub officer Ben Williams instructed a BA crew to standby along with entry control whilst other firefighters checked externally around the building. Round the back of the building the ground was very uneven; this would prove difficult to plumb a ladder to the correct orientation. Within a minute a call was heard over the radios from one of the lads at the rear of the building "Sub, we've got smoke issuing from a couple of cracked windows on the ground and first floors." The Sub officer instructed that crew to find a point of entry, which was actually difficult to find. The old Cliffe Hydro was, in certain areas, very heavily boarded up. The Sub also ordered breaking in tools to be brought to one of the doors. "Right then I want BACO set up at the rear of the premises and two BA started up." Me and Craig Long were the waiting BA wearers off of 021; and we started up. 022 was now in attendance with Sub O Derrin in charge, he heard the message and ordered two BA wearers from 022 to join us at the control point. Our team's brief was to enter the building and carry out a left-hand search of the ground floor area to locate and extinguished the fire BUT to take extreme caution and be aware of loose ceilings, loose or missing floorboards, loose masonry, hypodermic needles and the likes. During the brief another couple of firefighters were stripping multiple layers of tightly nailed and screwed wood panels from a door at ground floor level. They ended up axing and sledge-hammering the last few boards to create a half-decent gap for us. Craig and I climbed through the gap whilst trying to negotiate the cylinders on our backs through this gap. I gathered up loads of hosereel tubing and mustered it inside the door so that we could cover a good distance without running out of hosereel. Craig grabbed the branch (nozzle) then we began our search. We walked quite casually through the big ex-dining room which its high window's offered adequate light and a bonus of no smoke in the area, the flooring was still strong too. We both continued to search other rooms, halls and a kitchen which led us through other doors to lure us deeper into the darkening hotel. We heard that the second BA crew had entered the building to assist us. We found ourselves in a narrow corridor which was extremely dark. We checked rooms off the corridor but located no fire OR smoke as yet. "Craig, I can feel heat on my legs mate. It's got to be the other side of this partition wall."

Craig agreed and we continued to search to try and find a way to the next room without requesting a sledgehammer. We snaked back on ourselves down through another narrow corridor which took us through a door halfway down on the right. We carried out a door check and sprayed the upper part of the door with water to check for heat level; the water ran straight down without steaming off indicating that there was no heat on the other side, although there was smoke emitting from underneath and around the door, we obviously had no sense of smell due to wearing BA. I cracked the door ajar and Craig reported smoke within an area that resembled another corridor. BACO now asked for a 'Sitrep' (situation report). I informed the BACO to wait and I would get back with a sitrep shortly. The further we both continued down this corridor the thicker the smoke was. As we checked and opened another door we located a fire in the middle of the room, it looked like a large sofa bed alight.........and just about to be extinguished by another crew already there! "How did you get in?" I asked the crew. They stepped aside and pointed over their shoulders at the large open glass door at the side of the building which was originally covered in brambles and other vegetation, then continued to steal our thunder by knocking out the fire. I lifted the radio to my face mask.

"BA Control from BA 1, we are with BA team 2. Fire located, looks like a sofa-bed, now extinguished, over."

The second crew now withdrew and we remained with the other crew to check around the room. There was evidence of homeless people using the building as a 'squat'. A small table, a small chair, a large sofa-bed, (now cremated) and a 2-seater sofa. Also spotted were a few bottles of alcohol, tobacco and lighting equipment. Once happy that the fire was out we and the remaining crew went outside to open air and all headed back to clean and make-up the equipment. The Police were now in attendance so we left the scene in their hands.

FIRE – AGRICULTURAL

O ne sunny Friday afternoon both pumps were called to a barn fire at a location on the outskirts of the town known as Two Potts. 021 had just left the station with all guns blazing (excuse the pun) and 022 sat in silence as the lads started to clamber into the back. Today the station was short of drivers so Sub officer Derrin, being a trained emergency driver also, jumped into the driver's seat with leading firefighter McGovern as OIC. As a full crew we headed off following 021's route. Terry weaved through the Friday afternoon traffic and as we approached the road to where the farm was located we saw a drifting bank of thick brown/grey smoke wafting across the valley through the copse ahead. "We got ourselves a Barn boys!" Terry shouted back from the driver's seat. I was riding the BA3 position and Jim Stone BA2. I was gazing out at the smoke just thinking what another sodding barn fire we've got and on such a great summer's day. I wanted to strip back into my shorts and T-shirt which I was wearing just ten minutes before, not thick heavy fire kit with running bottoms on underneath (Brigade regulation was that if in shorts, the firefighter must wear full leg covering before donning fire leggings, this is a protection policy from heat in case the legs get burnt from radiated heat through the fire leggings. Most firefighters kept a pair of tracksuit leggings with their fire kit).

I was still gazing out of the window thinking that this would be a 'dragging and pulling burning hay apart all day' job, I looked across at the crew and notice that Jim had donned his BA set, he then turned to me and nodded as if to say *'quick get a set on'*. I went to grab mine (not to miss out on a wear) when I noticed the firefighter next to me had clocked on to Baggy's sneaky BA wear move and got his BA straps over his shoulders. Oh well, he was entitled to wear I suppose. Jim leant across "I did try to get your attention but you were in a world of your own." he laughed. We turned into the short inclined drive and pulled up behind 021 that was now in attendance and had its pump screaming away. A stonewalled barn, containing a van and bales of hay was 'going well' in and beyond the barn, but attached to the barn was another area containing cattle that the farmer had just released out of the rear door. These beasts strolled out coughing and spluttering, one looked particularly bad as it stumbled about before laying down near a wall, its tongue lolled out whilst it rasped and gulped for air trying to rid the acrid smoke. Steve grabbed the 'MARS (resuscitator) and jogged over to the calf, which in turn allowed Stevie to administer oxygen by clamping the oxygen therapy mask with his hand over the calf's mouth. The oxygen cleared its lungs as we saw life seep back into the animal. It then pulled its face away. Steve grabbed the MARS and stood back. The calf slowly stood up, looked at us for a second, turned and ran off to join the others in the field. "Well done Stevie. Nice one mate." I said giving him a pat on the back. He acknowledged this with his usual wide smile.

He saved the calf from smoke inhalation and why not? It's a living thing after all, we have a job to do, to save LIFE-any life, and property and these animals are the farmer's livelihood.

Steve actually achieved the same result via the same method

on a larger heifer on another barn fire a few years after this job. Me and a few others formed a team of 'drag-forkers' using drag forks to move the burning and smouldering hay about so that the jet from the hosereel could penetrate deep into the fire to guarantee a complete extinguishment. Sometimes the smoke was that dense that the optical and nasal sinuses open up acutely which results in streaming tears and mucus accompanied with constant coughing which to the point that we all ended up wearing BA (got there eventually Jim!).

Three o'clock one Sunday afternoon we were requested for a 'make-up' at a farm in the area known as Arlington. The call was to back-up fire crews from Barnstaple and Combe Martin at a large barn on fire. We were ordered to rendezvous (RV) near the entrance to the farm on an adjoining road.

022 with Sub O Derrin as OIC, arrived at the RV where we were met by an officer. He walked over to Terry's window as we leant out of the others looking at the smoke plume emitting from the farm below a track. "Aright Tel? Right, can you take your crew back up that road" he pointed, "and carry out a bit of 'hydrant duty' until the Police get here?" the hydrant was slap –bang in the middle of a narrow road with a standpipe and hydrant key attached and a 70mm hose supplying the crews down the road at the farm.

Terry acknowledged this then give us all a look of 'a make-up' and they want us to babysit a hydrant!' look on his face. I was with him on this. Great, we'll just sit here then. We traced back the hose to the hydrant and made sure that any traffic was diverted down another road. Jack placed a blue-flashing warning light next to the hydrant then joined the rest of us next to the pump observing the spoke plume billowing up near the end of the road. The police were busy elsewhere but turned up when they could. They set proper official diversions in place as they set 'road closed' signs up. They then told us that we were free to continue.

Terry radioed the Stn O, the OIC of the fire-ground, to make him aware that we were now available. The Stn O got back to him via the radio. "Thanks Terry. Um. If you can just hold there for a short while we will get you down here to relieve a crew from firefighting shortly ok? Oh yeah, and I've ordered fish and chips to the fire-ground, I'll make sure you get some!" I thought, *oh well, free lunch out of it if not anything else.* We did receive the food and had time to eat it whilst awaiting the call to go down to the farm. When the Stn O said 'shortly' he actually meant an hour; as that's when we saw a fire appliance leave the farm's entrance and we were called down.

On entering the farm yard we were faced with, what was, a barn (an area of 20 metres by 15 metres) which had been involved in a collapse which had left corrugated metal sheets from the walls and the roof all over the area, which the farmer was using one of his tractor's to push these out of the way. There were burning straw and hay bales that were breaking down and an old tractor on fire. A small section of barn which was used as an animal feed store was still standing, although very hazardously. A jet was being played into parts of the fire with no real urgency, this jet was fed from Barnstaple's pump whilst being supplement from the lonely hydrant up on the road. We walked over to the crew and asked what their plan of action was. "Ain't a lot left is there?" Mick said to them. One of their guys nodded to the burning mass of agricultural detritus "we've scaled down to one jet, the rest might slowly burn out. Just watching wind direction as it could blow it over the road. The farmer's told us that he's not bothered about the contents now as the barn is knackered as well as its contents and he shan't be using it again will he?" We then set up a jet and took over as the other pumps slowly whittled away from the scene.

The farmer and his wife were a lovely couple. She supplied lots of refreshment such as cold and hot drinks, biscuits, cake. Great stuff! As the sun slipped down below the high treeline the farmer brought out several chairs and sun-loungers for us to take a rest on whilst working in 'shifts' in order to quench the flames and reduce the billowing smoke. "Here boys, I got fertiliser in that store over there." The farmer pointed with concern. "Forgot all about that." A couple of us managed to risk a passage across to the store to move several bags away from the fire as these could be toxic and cause some respiratory distress and discomfort. The store, that wasn't involved directly by fire, succumbed to the twisting strain and heat after an hour.

Daylight was fading rapidly now. So the plan was to work a couple of firefighters at a time, one on the jet and one or two using drag-forks to break apart the tangled deep mess of hay and straw, which was now nearly level and not resembling round bales anymore. We would swap round and the 'workforce' would take a rest whilst the others took part. As darkness enveloped the scene. Large embers and tongues of flame were contrasting their red and orange colours against the darkening backdrop. "Right, swap over." The Sub ordered. Myself and Mick got up and made our way over to the mass of burning fodder. Mick had the jet first and I was joined by Mike Holt, we used drag forks to good effect; opening up the tangled mass whilst Mick gave it a good blast with the jet deep down to extinguish the flames within. We took turns on the jet then was relieved from the firefighting by the others. The three of us then collapse on the ad-hoc seating arrangement and drank tea and shovelled in copious amounts of food. The farmer was still tending to his cattle (which were all ok) and other tasks whilst we got on with ours.

"WHOA, BLOODY HELL THAT'S HOT." Can you get another jet out lads, quick! Whoa, ow, sodding fire." One of our 'drag-forkers' had ventured onto an area of burning hot embers which he could feel discomfort within his fire boots, then pain within them as the heat was prolonged and intense! He was hopping back over to the pump as the pump operator ran out a jet and sprayed his feet with the cold water. "Oh that's it. That's better mate, phew" the pump operator then placed the jet on the floor with the branch half-cracked in case anyone else needed their boots cooling-which they did! We laughed at this guy, and the other one which came trotting over to the second jet to rid the heat also. We were next to play. So we headed over the fire and got to work covering a large area rapidly. I was on the jet, whilst my fellow firefighters were running off every so often to cool their feet. We swapped and I started to move into the mass again with the drag-fork. *'What's the matter with them, it's a bit warm but not hot, it's not as if their bare-footed'* I thought. I worked the fork for another minute and then felt discomfort. I placed my feet under the working jet then cracked on with moving the straw and hay, only for roughly a minute, then searing heat was felt again. "Wow, sodding hell I've got to go" I was next in line to witness the foot torture and rapidly headed for the second jet to cool my boots down. "You weren't kidding lads were you?" I just received shaking heads and smiles from them. Through the night we worked. The Sub and I got up to use drag-forks to break down a burning mass at the far corner of the barn. We dragged most of it apart whilst others were setting up lighting equipment. We both made our way along the waist-high wall, the heat was so intense here that I could feel my face tingling. As we leaned lightly on the wall I could feel a 'give' in it; a slight play in the wall as it was loosened accompanied with an evident crack. I warned Terry of the danger and we decided that this was now a no go area, and we left the cover of the wall due to it being unsafe. We grabbed a brew back at the edge of the barn, I took my gloves of then went to take my fire helmet off. "Shit!" I protested and threw the helmet onto a tyre. "That's piping hot that lid." (Helmet) I gave it a few minutes then picked it up and noticed that the fire service badge on the front was only half the size. It had melted the bottom half of the badge and shrivelled it. We continued the 'shifts' until daylight. We dragged our bedraggled bodies and kit back on the pump and back to home station to clear up. We all looked like pandas with deep black eyes where we had been rubbing them to rid the sweat. Our uniforms and the station muster bay all stank of smoke. Even after several showers you could still smell the smoke and see a tracing of carbon round our eyes. I did receive a new fire helmet badge.

That was a large barn fire in which the farmers were grateful for our attendance. Only a small amount of his livelihood 'went up' very quickly in the barn, at least his cattle and other farm machinery was saved. A barn fire is like a thatched roof fire, it can catch and spread very quickly and take an absolute age to slow down and extinguish. That's rural firefighting for you.

BNEC – SCOTLAND

T he BNEC team left North Devon and England to cross the border into bonnie Scotland for the second of the Nationals of the BNEC. We stayed overnight at a travel lodge in the north of England before heading off the next day into Scotland. Well we were not near any City so no pub-crawl, so it would be a bite to eat with a few jars in a quite local pub not far from our temporary accommodation. We mustered at the reception foyer at 7pm and all walked up to the main road in search of a pub. Terry spotted a pub in the not so far distance. We piled in the pub which was quite sparse of customers, played pool and generally had a chat about the challenge and enjoyed a Bite to eat and a few beers, then for the trudge back and a good night's sleep ready for the morning.

30th July 1999. We arrived in Glasgow, the weather looked fine again. We found our classical plush 'Thistle Hotel' in the City and booked in, we then sought a curry house in the early evening and took in the sights and sounds of Glasgow. We took things easy and then got our heads down for the challenge the next morning.

The early alarm sounded to mentally drag us from our slumber and after a shower and breakfast we headed off to Hamilton Fire Station in Strathclyde. All RTC arenas all look the same at the Nationals within lots of barriers placed in positions to create multiple performance areas. Our team were not on until the afternoon, so again, we took opportunity to look around the exhibition stalls and watched other Brigades doing their stuff in the arenas. Lots of sponsorship companies were 'flying their flags'. Big Company's such as Bristol (uniforms), Holmatro and Hurst (extrication tools and equipment) also other Emergency services were all attending this event.

After a spot of lunch we made our way to our area to get kitted up and prepared for a safety brief. Our slot was at 3pm. We kitted up, listened to the safety brief, checked our equipment area then watched the team before us carrying out their scenario. Kent Fire and rescue were just before us. They extricated their casualties just shy of the twenty minute mark. We then prepared for our scenario. Just after 3pm we jogged into the arena to be presented with an estate car on its roof..........but crushed down quite low (pancaked) as if it had been in a high speed rollover; with the driver trapped. We stabilised quickly and effectively. The driver's door had buckled out so a least Jim and Mick could reach in to check and monitor all clinical signs. They were told by the judges what trauma the patient has sustained. Ben liaised with the medics and us, as tool men, to establish just how to extract the driver.

The front was quite badly crushed but allowing a bit more space to the rear of this car. Due to this scenario being a rollover we obviously needed to protect the C-spine and start thinking about spine management as this casualty needed to come out on a longboard. Ben decided that it would be out of the question and time-sapping if we cut the side out as we would have to use several pieces of equipment to shore the vehicle floor up which would also get in the way. This method would de-stabilise and weaken the car too. I climbed in to discover that we had some room in the front of the car which maybe two firefighters could just about fit into with awkward manipulation. I left the medics to it whilst the medical judge looked on, I clambered out. "Shit, this is going to be a right sod" I said to Ben and Terry. Ben suggested that we remove the rear door by cutting away the hinges; get a hydraulic ram ready to the rear of the car and actually then place the ram in place to keep the car steady also to prevent further collapse. We connected both tools as Ben explained to the medics what we were doing. Terry and I managed to break the rear door's lock, which had been deformed slightly, and force the door down to open (as the car was on its roof). Terry then used the Hurst cutters to shear through the hinges in seconds whilst I supported the door, removed it out of the way and immediately placed the ram into position; placed just off centre as so we could maintain space for the casualty removal.

I energised the ram then placed the foot of it against a flat block on the ground and raised the ram's piston to meet with the sill next to the lock where the door would close onto. This done, we re-checked stabilisation to which I duly slid the longboard in through the rear of the car. Jim indicated that they, the medics, had the casualty stable and C-spine collar fitted. They had worked really well especially that the casualty was hanging upside down in the seatbelt! Ben gave me the nod "Ok Bags, clear to go mate." I wiggled through the interior of the car and made my way to the front I then grabbed the end of the longboard that Terry had passed in and I heaved it up alongside my body. Jim had passed over control of the head to Mick who would now support the c-spine. I slowly rolled the back of the seat flat via the roller grip mechanism and supported the casualty. Another pair of hands joined mine from the left side; Terry had joined me to assist in taking the weight of the casualty, giving encouragement and advice as we worked. We gave Mick the nod and whilst we braced for the reaction and the weight Mick reached through and released the seatbelt. With a sudden weight transfer we carefully lowered the driver onto the board, I took over the head from Jim then shuffled back on my knees to get behind the board and control the head further. Jim and Mick now ran round to the rear to assist with the board as it carefully but surely emerged from the back. Between myself and Terry we cautiously manoeuvred the driver into the middle of the board, Terry placed the head-blocks either side of the patient's head. I quickly re-positioned my hands to accommodate this. I could see the judges at either side of the car looking in at the work going on within this confined space. It was hot inside the car and I kept feeling the need to keep rubbing my head on my shoulder of my fire tunic to rid the sweat. Our medics had the longboard straps ready outside to attach them when we were out as we would have more space to work.

Inside we were both huffing and puffing dragging the board and the driver along the inside of roof of the car. "Nearly there Baggy, good work nearly out." Terry whispered. All we needed to do now was to get the driver completely out of the vehicle and the clock would stop. The driver was no longer trapped but effort was needed to pull his weight along the inside of the car as we could only get two firefighters inside the crumpled wreck, just! "Watch the ram Terry." I shouted across to him as we neared the opening behind us. Time had caught up with us and the whistle sounded whilst we were only two foot from exiting the car. The challenge is marked on full medical extrication from us turning up to when the trapped patient is outside the vehicle, that's when the clock stops and not when the casualty/s are cut free and still in the car as judges want to observe our handling skills also. Despite the awkwardness of the scenario we nearly achieved full removal of the driver but the twenty minutes beats us. This of course was competition mode, in the real world with an actual real scenario we wouldn't be timed but would still be under pressure to remove collision victims rapidly but safely.

Anyway, the challenge was won by a northern brigade. Well done to them as they and the rest of the teams put in an amazing effort throughout the day. We topped off the challenge that day by guzzling a few beers in the evening.......as per usual! But well deserved. Then on to find the hotel in a haze of vision and all duly drifted off to sleep with the distant haze of city life and sirens still on-going outside.

Overall I had found the British National Extrication Challenge to be.....well, challenging. I had met some great characters and worked with an excellent team both within the team itself and back on the drill and fire-grounds. Barnstaple fire station decided that they would like to start an RTC team to compete for a few years. Ilfracombe did not apply for competition again as we now had a few challenges under our belts and we thought that we ought to let another team have a go. We still then had two North Devon teams in the running. A year later the team at station 01 Barnstaple won their first regional challenge and went on to represent Devon fire and rescue service at the national challenge in Northern Ireland.

A DANGEROUS SHOUT

I was woken from my comatose-sleep; it was one thirty in the morning. The pager had a way of doing that sometimes. Two lights were illuminated outside the appliance bays doors; red and blue, indicating that both pumps were required for this emergency call. The first pump had the last guy jumping on so I ran over to 022 and took a seat next to the other man in the middle, the BACO/BA 3. I was now BA 4 so I would be the 'runner', running out covering jets, hosereels taking part as a ladder crew if required along with BA 3, as the BACO would set up from the first pump. A covering jet is several lines of hose that's connected to make one line with a branch at the business end and laid out near the entrance of the building; this is then charged with water. If anything goes wrong inside or outside then this jet can be hauled into the building or used outside immediately if required. Harry was last man on slamming the door shut as we watched 021 storm out of the doors, then we followed swiftly behind. We heard Sub officer Williams book out on their radio as they stated that they had a crew of six and were mobile. On our pump Sub officer Derrin booked out with a crew of six also. I turned to Jack "What we got mate?" Jack shouted over the roaring engine "Flat fire. Larkstone

Terrace." Harry looked at the crew. "We went to this place last night didn't we at half past nine?* that first floor flat that was on fire? What's the number on the tip sheet terry?" Harry shouted confusingly to the OIC. Terry revealed the number of the address. "Yeah, that's the place we had last night." Harry expressed in part confusion part despair. We heard over the radio that 021 were in attendance, "*021 in attendance, third floor well alight, make pumps six, over.*"

We were fifteen seconds behind and we saw the fire from the top of the road. Harry cursed as his tunic zip got stuck a third of the way up the zip mechanism and he couldn't budge it. He couldn't go in as this would have been dangerous because he was not fully protected from the heat. As he struggled with the zip he shouted across to me "You'll have to get a set on Bags, sodding zip's stuck." "OK mate" I grabbed the set which was housed behind me and dragged it onto my back. Harry let me out whilst Jack exited the nearside door along with my BA mate who I'd not really acknowledged as yet. Lots of orders were being yelled from the OIC's. I looked up at the fire on the upper floors of the four story building and saw a fierce well established fire that awaited us. I made my way over to a firefighter, Carl, who had set up the entry control point outside the garden gate, separated from the entrance to the large, tall building by a twenty foot path. The first BA team from 021 had just entered the building with a hosereel after handing their tallies to Carl and obtaining their brief.

* I was off-duty on the previous evening so missed the first call to the flat on fire which, by all accounts, was severely damaged by fire.

My BA team-mate was Matt, not long out of his probationary period; he's a good lad and should be ok as long he doesn't let his excitement and adrenaline run away with him. We got the order to 'start up' and received our brief, then swiftly handed in our tallies before we entered the ground floor entrance. No-one at this stage was sure if there were persons reported or not. No smoke met us on the ground and first floors; we began to heave lots of hosereel off from 022, and placed the tubing up through the middle of the stairwell as we ascended to the upper floors to save dragging it around the stair banister instead. On the third floor we could hear the fire on the next floor up and witnessed the glow as we made our way up the stairway. Fire Embers floated down past us. Last set of stairs and we could now feel the heat. The top floor flat was well alight and the atmosphere was extremely smoky, but light from the fire was offering quite good visibility if we got down low. We arrived at the boots of the first team as they knelt on the landing attacking the fire with a hosereel jet. They moved over slightly in order for us to accompany them in the firefight. We all faced the entrance to the flat with our backs to the inside of the front of the building with a dormer window above our heads behind us. The first BA crew had knocked down some fire on the edge of the landing to ceiling level. The dormer was quite unstable so we had to keep an eye on it. The whole flat was decomposing in what the Fire Service called 'Pyrolysis' this is where a fire heats up at and along the ceiling level, heat starts to radiate down, in turn heating up any furniture below the flames, so the wallpaper starts to smoulder and burn, then the sofa, armchair, beds, table, ashtray, telephone, TV, rugs, carpet, the lot. This can be extremely dangerous as this can cause a 'flashover' where everything burst into flame simultaneously all of a sudden, catching anyone out in the vicinity. This flat was alight and as we could see from the landing stairs everything underneath the lowering smoke layer was pyrolising. A quick check on that dormer then we concentrated high pressured jets into the flat. The smoke slightly dissipated allowing the intense angry flames to light the whole flat entrance and hall which I could clearly see that the lounge was on the right and ahead of us and a bedroom on the left through another open door, we could not have advanced further in at the time as the fire was raging like a wall holding us back, the heat stung our faces and we experienced an continuous intense heat build-up. We slowly knocked the fire back into the flat, as we did I decided to shuffle forward on my knees (always ideal to be low down as we had more vision and the temperature was cooler, not a lot, but slightly cooler.) I actually knocked out a significant area of fire in the lounge whilst the other crew tackled the bedroom, I continued to inch my way in although I knew that the fire had probably broken through the roof.

A Leading Firefighter from 021's crew bounded up the stairs and remained halfway down the last flight to the third floor and shouted up "Baggy turn your branch down, water's entering the flat below." I couldn't work this statement out. *'Water going in the flat below?'* what's he talking about.......So?! I shouted down to him, "it's going like the clappers up here, probably gone through the roof by now anyway. Sod below, get a jet up here!" The Leading firefighter then disappeared back down the stairs hopefully to return with a jet. A quick check on that dormer window, a bit dodgy but will last for a bit longer. Still inching myself in alongside my crewmate we made slow progress in this relentless battle. The first crew were now fighting the fire within the bedroom to the lounge with their hosereel jet. I adjusted to full jet and temporarily knocked back the fire deep in the lounge. I quickly adjusted the branch again to spray/jet to knock out hotspot areas around us to make it safe then adjusted back to full jet to hit the distant ceilings, walls and floors. We achieved a desired effect but the intensity of the fire was such that it reared up time after time. A third BA crew joined us and waited near the top of the third floor stairs as four firefighters were enough on that small landing. We must have been fighting this fire for fifteen to twenty minutes now and having a bloody hard fight. "Check on the surrounding lads especially that sodding dormer too!" I shouted with ever more cautionary awareness. This didn't feel right. We all gained approximately six foot advancement only. I hit at the fiery monster again to see if it did bite back but it did respite for a minute, then Andrew, from the first team, who had a quick look around at our surroundings, tapped me on the shoulder and stopped me from going any further into this unrelenting inferno while he pointed upwards, I stopped immediately and looked up to where he was pointing. "OH SHIT!" A large metal water tank was fully exposed through the fire damaged ceiling and it seemed to be very unstable to the point that I could see it physically moving on ONE single roof joist "OH THAT IS NOT GOOD! GET BACK; GET BACK OUT OF THE FLAT. IT'S UNSTABLE UP THERE!" I shouted to the lads whilst also mentioning the menacing dormer unit. That was well spotted by Andrew, I slapped him on the back with acknowledgment and we moved back out onto the landing. I looked up at the dormer window again; the whole unit seemed to be moving and creaking. This still didn't feel right at all. I was thinking that this had gone through the roof now but couldn't see through the flames to actually tell, the dormer could go at any time and there were six BA wearers up here and maybe more below checking the flats and this lot could end up on us at any minute. I saw that one of the first crew was giving a situation report to the BACO. Sweat started to sting my eyes but dried quickly via the heat through my BA mask. This was now a dire situation that we were in. Jets still trained on the fire, the guys outside must have got a clearer picture of the situation. An OIC came bounding up the stairs. "Right lads, knock off let's get out of here, the fire is through the roof and it looks unstable." Our eyes and thoughts were not playing tricks on us in this intense heat.

All six of us didn't hang about and with our hose lines we started to follow the OIC down the stairs, I then heard short sharp blasts on a whistle outside then another whistle, then many whistles, then a couple of whistle sounds from inside the building on the lower levels.

These repeated short sharp blasts are to warn Firefighters and other agencies that something is not right, i.e. collapse imminent, so firefighters must evacuate if still within the building and others need to get away far from the building as in NOW!

All firefighters carry whistles in their tunic for this purpose and when one person blows theirs then everyone should sound theirs too to enhance the sound as to ensure everyone can hear this warning and take action. Blimey, it seemed longer getting down the bloody stairs than it did coming up. What was making it worse through the reverberating whistle sounds was whether we'd get out in time. We walked as fast as we could with BA on our backs and as not to fall and be delayed in the evacuation, through the burning embers that dropped down the stairwell and all around us. The whistles sounded more intense now as we left the front entrance into the night air. That's when I heard it, a cracking sound above us, I kept walking with the lads but kept glancing back to the position that we had just left on the upper floor. Part of the roof above that flat started to collapse, it wasn't like in the movies where the actors leave the building and within a second everything is reduced to dust,; but it wasn't far off that scenario. By the time we reached the gate a good chunk of the roof from front to back collapsed with a loud thundering crunch; this also fell onto the landing that we were knelt three minutes before. The dormer window hadn't quite fell right through but fell backward part the way into the building and stopped at an awkward angle threatening to follow the roof down. It hung dangerously. We booked in at BA control, collected our tallies and were pointed in the direction of the BA cleaning area, which was on a ground floor patio area of a property two doors up. Several fire appliances were now at the scene along with the specialist appliances such as the Bronto and Incident support unit (ISU from Barnstaple) and Incident Command unit (ICV from our station) along with several appliances from other stations. We started to prepare our sets and changed our BA cylinders which were now low on air and started to chat to a few of the lads from Barnstaple who had been in the lower rooms prior to the evacuation, they were also cleaning their sets. Someone mentioned that the roof had now gone in and another stated that it was a bloody good job that it had as there should not now be any further danger posed from above if we had to move up to the upper floors again. Sub officer Derrin came over to our crew as we were just checking the newly-cleaned and serviced sets. "You lot done with your sets?" Without looking up we quickly finished the checks. "Yep, all done" I said. "Right lads, my lot, I want you all to check into BA control as I need to commit you inside the building again." I could hear sirens at a distance at all directions racing toward the scene to assist in tackling the blaze.

"Right listen in lads" the Sub sternly retorted. "I want you to go back in, up to the second floor, pick up the jet which has been taken in previously and fight the fire in the third floor flat." Matt and I were still looking up at the wild flames menacingly luring us to duel with it like a prisoner at a window trying to escape. I repeated the brief back to Terry in acknowledgment. We booked in at BA entry control and followed the red rubber 45mm hose which was transferring water from 021 to the enemy upstairs. We both pounded up the stairs avoiding previous debris from roofing materials, plasterwork and rubble. I noticed a BA crew on the first floor tackling a small fire in behind a doorway of a flat with a hosereel, the flat was probably the one that was on fire earlier in the evening. I nodded to them and proceed up to the third floor where we both experienced heat and embers of the burning compartments above us. We teamed up with a Barnstaple crew which had just come down from extinguishing fire on the stairs which had probably ignited after the collapse. We approached the burning flat, Matt keenly grabbed the jet and I gathered up some hose behind us. Both of us knelt by the door to the flat. I cracked the door open slightly to witness a roaring fire behind it then quickly shut it to compile a plan of attack. I shouted to Matt "Right mate, I'll crack the door again and you open the jet and give it a bloody good drink through the gap. Then I'll open the door further and we'll give it all we've got to knock it down ok?" he gave the thumbs up and the door opened slightly. With jet open Matt swirled the water round one side of the room. I opened the door wider bit by bit then let go of it completely letting the water knock it wide open supported I supported Matt with the jet whilst we hit all areas of the flat. A jet of water entered the flat's entrance from our right; I looked across to find a Barnstaple BA crew supporting us with a hosereel. The fire in the ceiling was slowly knocked back and brought under control but it looked like there was a huge hole in the ceiling. This was the flat directly below the area where the roof collapsed. We achieved an impressive knock down of the fire initially by using the jet along with the hosereel. I looked back and gathered more hose-line then all of a sudden the hose-line went taught and my supporting hand slipped off matt's shoulder. I looked back to see he started to make rapid progress into the flat with fire still either side of him. I gripped the hose tightly to prevent him going further. His mind was having other thoughts whilst fighting this fire. "Matt! Get back here!" I desperately shouted. He was then grabbed by another firefighter. "What ya doing mate? Fight it from the door way. Knock it back from here. It's well alight and slow progression" He turned to me "There may be people in there." he pleaded. We had no reports of persons reported. One of the Firefighters shouted over to him "It's not worth it mate. In reality if there's anyone in there, they're dead." The Barnstaple crew let us know that they are down to their safe air working margin and needed to withdraw. Matt and I cracked on with the jet and extinguished a significant area of fire in the flat from the hall and inner door.

We kept an anxious eye on our air and reported to BA control that we will soon also need to withdraw. Within five minutes a fresh BA crew were sent to relieve us. We could hear on our radios that a fire was going well on the fourth floor and roof again.

We got to the BACO and shut down our sets I gave the BACO our de-brief of where we had been and what we had done and grabbed three bottles of water, I placed one on the wall for the BACO and threw one over to Matt, he done well up there. I looked up to scan the building while I gulped the cold fresh water eagerly. The building looked a sorry state with fire visually emanating out of the roof and upper floors again. On a flat roof next door I saw a Leading firefighter who had got to the flat roof via a ladder and was attempting to extinguish a fire with a hosereel through a third floor window externally. We went to change our cylinders when I noticed the crew which had come to relieve us five minutes ago were coming back out of the front door. I passed Jack, our BACO who now had help from a BA 'Supervisor' who mans the BA radios for him. I gave him a nod "what's the score Jack?" He looked at me then back to his board as he returned the tallies to the withdrawing wearers. "We're going Defensive mate. Too dodgy to mess about inside." I laughed "You're telling me! See you later." When we initially turned up we entered the building and attacked the fire from inside wearing BA and using hose to extinguish the heart of the fire at close quarters; this is known as 'Offensive mode' if the building starts to collapse or is unsafe then the officers will decide to pull the crews out and we will attack it from outside with jets trained in through the roof and windows, keeping us safe. This is known as 'Defensive mode.' A 'transitional mode' was when a fire was attacked from both inside and outside of the building. I followed Matt to service our sets for the last time that morning. I put my set back on the pump and noticed a pump driving around the back of the building in order to support the firefighters there either by support with another jet or ladder. I jumped down off the pump and could hear other appliances screaming away pumping water to various jets being supplemented by street hydrants.

"Ladder crew, ladder crew" an OIC shouted I threw my empty bottle of water on the pump and since I had not been tasked a job I jogged over to assist. Matt was elsewhere doing something else. Four of us gathered at the OIC "I want a 1.3.5. ladder up to the third floor window, I will then get a couple of fellas up there with a jet working from the head of the ladder to knock out the fire within that room and up through the broken floor. We're going to have to manhandle the ladder over that hedge and wall in order to get the heel in to achieve a straight pitch to the building! Right, get to work." With all crews now working in Defensive mode we managed to transfer the heavy ladder over the walled-hedge and, tactfully pitch it against the building. Some crews, including myself, were due a cuppa and a bite to eat, we were getting tired.

We wearily trudged over to the Incident support unit that was preparing hot food like soup and beans and sausages which came in packs which are heated by the support crew and handed out with polythene serving trays with a plastic knife and fork. The British Red Cross were also in attendance. They do a marvellous job attending the now homeless people and support the firefighters by also supplying food. Their range of food was more variable with all sorts of food and drink from hot chocolate to coke-cola from chocolate bars to burgers.

If you look long enough you will see a line of firefighters move from the queue at the Incident support unit over to the British red-cross van! The Salvation Army was another amazing organisation that used to attend fires to loyally serve and help fire victims and firefighters alike. Great people serving society nationally and internationally.

A good time to mention, due to a large fire and the amount of BA sets used, is that of the Brigade's 'handyman' (technician). Based out of station 01 Barnstaple he was the stalwart of logistical matters.

When BA cylinders needed replenishing, he was there gathering up all the empties, loading them on his van and returning them to our station, 02, to refill them via the air compressor (which was fitted at our station) he would then return the full cylinders to fire ground with any other ancillary equipment that had been asked for. This task would obviously be carried out at large fires all over North Devon; so he kept very busy on these large jobs. During daylight hours he was kept busy through normal logistical matters throughout the North of the county also.

Back to the fire. After our fill we returned back to the building and grabbed a jet to train water externally upon the fire until daybreak. The bronto then played its water jet down from its monitor high above acting as a water tower. At daybreak the stubborn Dormer window unit was still resting back over the collapsed area and had not collapsed along with the remainder of the roof. The bronto was now just dampening down as all signs of fire was now extinguished and crews were hitting hot-spots. The bronto knocked-off its water and re-positioned against the dormer unit. Some surrounding loose debris was cut away and then a ceiling hook was used to collapse the unit, to no avail. A line then attached to the unit was used to pull against the frame intermittently in a rocking motion in the hope to loosen the whole unit. After a while the dormer unit cracked and snapped and was pulled from the building. Later that morning some crews, including myself, went back into the smouldering structure to look at the remaining area and to check the fire damage. The flat on the third floor, in which we were joined by the Barnstaple crew and fought the fire from the doorway, was completely burnt-out. In fact as we poked I head into the lounge and went quite clammy as I observed a massive hole in the floor with wood and other debris sticking out from it, it was a good job matt didn't go any further earlier. The floor in the lounge had collapsed helped by the collapse of the upper floors. We did not bother going further up to the upper floors as we knew the fate of that flat and the roof.

A fire investigating officer (FIO) had been in attendance and was investigating the fire along with a structural engineer. We left the fire-ground at around midday, with two relief crews remained at the scene for most of the following day.

Another intimidating shout was when both pumps turned out to a fire 11pm on a Saturday evening in December. '**021 – 022. HOUSE FIRE, POSSIBLE PERSONS REPORTED.**' The house was a bungalow located four miles out of town. When we approached the road leading to the address we could see that this bungalow had a well-developed fire to the rear of the house and fire showing in the roof space. I was riding as BA2 and Tom was BA1 both on 021. On our arrival we stepped off the pump and heard 022 slightly skid to a halt a little further behind 021. Everyone on-scene was running about the fire-ground doing the necessary jobs. Matt ran past me and Tom as we were reporting to BACO. He had a large sledgehammer in his hands heading for the front door.

We booked in with BACO; Sub O Williams briefed us. "Right Boys, possible persons' take a hosereel in, firefight and search and rescue; I will get another team in with you as soon as poss." At the front door Matt had tried the UPVC door handle, it was locked with dead-bolts within the door. I carried out a radio check with BACO whilst looking through the glass at the fire within, someone opened up a hosereel jet onto the roof to allay some flames that were eagerly spreading along the roof.

Matt attacked the large double-glazed glass panel within the door itself as there were no windows open elsewhere. He managed to smash both layers of glass whilst calling out for a salvage sheet as so it could be placed over the lower lip of the panel to protect us as we climbed in through the door. I was thinking about the locked door;

does this mean the person's out or locked it up for the evening before retiring to bed? Tom checked the hosereel for water and directed the jet in through the open space in through the door to knock back the volatile advancing flames. He then scrambled through the open door panel. I gathered a few loops of hosereel then followed him through the door, I told Matt to keep the hose coming. I glanced at the lock on the inside and saw no key in place, that could mean something or nothing, but hopefully the occupant/s are out. As tom hit the flames within this small building I searched the kitchen to the right, I kept tom in view. The search revealed nothing; I then searched the dining room on the left which was filling with smoke but not too thick as not to see, nothing found. My radio crackled into life. "BA TEAM ONE FROM BACO. NEIGHBOURS HAVE REPORTED THAT AN ELDERLY GENT LIVES HERE ALONE, THEY'VE NOT SEEN HIM GO OUT AT ALL." I acknowledged this briefly, this still didn't mean if he was inside or not. We both advanced the hosereel working to good use knocking the flames back, the heat now building tremendously. Now standing in the lounge, we completed a search of the area, knocking things over as we clumsily but efficiently searched. Again nothing found.

We worked our way over to the left side of the bungalow where the fire was at its worse, this led to a bedroom that was on fire along one side of the room, tom knocked the flames back that were teasing around us and we both carried out a thorough search of the room, on the bed, under it, behind the doors, under the windows, in the wardrobes, the lot, as trained to do. Nothing. Hot embers were pouring down from the ceiling due to the fire in the roof. We left the bedroom and re-entered the lounge and searched it again, to double check. I could feel a spring like structure under my boots whilst checking the far corner of the room; I knelt down and trained my torchlight on it closely, It was a bed mattress; then I continued with a search of the immediate area again. Nothing. The smoke was clearing a little now as it was heading out towards the front door. I asked BA team two, that had now entered the property, to search the kitchen and dining rooms again. I knew they were absolutely clear, but I wanted them to check whilst they were in that area. The embers were raining down more frequently now To the right was a small bathroom which was lit by light from the flames but not on fire itself, the small room was in a recessed area, I quickly dashed in whilst tom extinguished some hotspots, nothing found. I stepped over the mattress in the lounge and looked up in the thinning smoke to the ceiling and found a massive hole. The mattress probably wasn't put in the lounge on the ground prior to the fire but had more than likely been on fire in the roof space and eventually burned through the ceiling from the roof space and landed on the lounge floor below, possibly? Tom and I both retreated to the hall and aimed the hosreel jet/spray at the ceiling to knock any loose material down and to cool the area. I could see intense flames within the roof space beyond the hole in the ceiling. Every once in a while the smoke would slightly clear and offer us a view of the ceiling which was red hot and cracking, shapes were forming in the ceiling plaster outlining unrecognisable items that were probably stored there that were now starting to burn through. BA team two confirmed nothing found in both kitchen and dining rooms, I informed BACO to tell the OIC that no persons were found. I was told that the roof had now become fully involved and we should think about withdrawing. A ladder crew had investigated the roof space from the outside and confirmed that the space within the roof was not another living area but looked like storage only. We looked up at the ceiling again whilst starting to head for the door when we felt large lumps of material hitting us from above and rebounding of our fire helmets. It felt extremely hot now and very smoky again. The ceiling was starting to crack and break up. BA team two had already withdrawn whilst we were stood in the hall knocking out hotspots and cooling the ceiling, then large parts of the ceiling started to fall along with various storage item from above. We change from professionals into an old comedy act as we proceeded faster and faster toward the front door. BANG. Another part of the ceiling fell in front of us, then another fell whilst on fire, tom was going to open up the hosereel on it, I place my hand across the hose, "Sod that mate, the whole roof's going well, we shouldn't be in here mate. I glanced up as we was nearing the front door, flames now raged over our heads that was the ceiling; everything was now spalling, cracking and falling.

The comedy act became more comical as we now ran the last fifteen or so feet to the door. Everything was collapsing. Evacuation whistles were sounding outside. "Shit, quick, get out bagger's!" tom said in a highly excited voice. He threw the branch of the hosereel through the open panel and that's when this comedy duo really took centre stage. We were now being hit by most things falling as the fire spread at ceiling level along the hall. Both at the same time we both entered the gap in the door, clawing at each other to get through, one leg still in the building, the other leg hanging outside the front door as we both attempted to squeeze through this gap which was not going to accommodate two firefighters wearing breathing apparatus at the same time! So, tom and I had filled this gap in the door accompanied with the remainder of the hosereel. We were pulling on the door and grabbing each other in desperation to take evasive action from the fiery torrent above. Carl ran across and gave us a hand out. It was like a cork out of a bottle. As I walked away from the bungalow over to the lawn I doubled over. Tom continued walking then turned to see me bent over shaking, he came back over to me. "Here, bags, you ok mate?" Even though I had air coming through my mask I couldn't get my breath quick enough. "What's up baggy, get your mask off mate." I stood up and looked at him with tears in my eyes. Tom looked concerned, "I know mate, that spooked me out and all" I eventually spoke through gasps letting out an almighty laugh in which I had been doing since we were hanging out of the door scrambling to get out. I couldn't stop laughing. "No, you daft sod I'm ok, it was us just now trying to squeeze through that door, cracked me right up!" I then doubled over again in fits of laughter. "Come on bags let's get over to BACO" I straightened up and we walked over to the entry control, shut down our sets and I had to dry my eyes with my tunic sleeve, which was now blackened with thick carbon deposits, which immediately turned my face into that of a panda, which started tom off laughing. I was still in fits of laughter and pointed to the BACO whilst looking at tom "you'll................you'll have to ....give him the debrief mate.............(more laughing)......I can't speak!!

Later in the early hours the roof fire was extinguished using a hosereel and main jet, then the roof succumbed to the fire and collapsed. On investigation, the fire seemed to have started in the roof space and burned through setting the contents of the main bungalow on fire. We were informed that the elderly gent was somewhere else safe and well.

'LADY BETTY' AND OTHER UNUSUAL EMERGENCIES

T he Fire Service, like other services are always in the public eye. People not only turn to us in the event of an emergency from a fire or other rescue, but also approach us for less taxing (and less stressful) public work such as fundraising and awareness-raising campaigns. We have carried out yearly charity car washes, several football, rugby, cricket and golfing events, Fire engine pulls from one end of the Town to the other inviting firefighters from other stations to also participate. We have washed and brushed down streets on the annual street cleaning mornings, attended fetes and even gave assistance to a local church in the way of fixing a new flagpole to the roof of the church above the belfry. At another event we were called on to help out with the annual vintage steam rally event. These excellent marvels of mobile steam engineering rendezvous at the town's sea front for the public to view them. In single file they head through the town sounding their steam whistles as they go and end up at the local swimming pool car park to reassemble once again. Once they gather at the seafront on the Saturday morning their tanks are usually quite low on water and they obviously need to produce steam to drive the piston and chain-driven axles in order to move. Their fuel supply of coal is plentiful being supplied from a constant supplier. But for water, for this event, the organisers contact the Fire Service to use our hoses to fill their tanks.

One Saturday morning we took 022 to the sea front to carry out the duty of filling or topping up their tanks, we would then leave them to do their thing and then meet them later at the other end for a top up, for them to continue further as they went on to their home towns and villiages. We were due to meet them for a top up at 5pm. At 4.30pm we were called to the swimming pool car park. Not for an early refill but an emergency call. '022 - *INCIDENT INVOLVING STEAM ENGINE - FIRE.*' So we responded in the customary fashion of blue lights and sirens. As we approached the car park we just saw a large gathering of steam engines and no obvious fire or smoke. The Sub spotted someone at the bottom end of the car park waving us down, so as we drove a wide circuit around the central group of engines and headed down to the edge of the car park, we then saw the problem, a large vintage steam engine, the 1902-built 'Lady Betty' from Somerset on its side on a grass verge up against a hedge producing lots of steam. The burning coal had shifted and the burning pile was close to the hedge. The Sub ordered a hosereel to be got to work to extinguish the moving contents of the coal box, so Jack, assisted by yours truly, squeezed against the hedge and the water tank and awkwardly got a water jet into and around the coal box to cool the hedge and majority of the hot mass before recovery attended and up-righted the vehicle.

It transpired that the steam engine toppled from a load-loader lorry as it was manoeuvring onto it. The driver and driver's mate jumped clear as the Lady Betty hit the ground. But they were unhurt.

We received calls to people shut in elevators on occasions. We get a person/s shut in lift, we attend, a couple of guys find the lift motor room whilst the others are opening the lift doors to ascertain what floors the lift cage is stuck between. In the motor room the brake is locked and the lift is manually wound up or down to a convenient floor for the trapped victim/s to be freed, Job done. People that are trapped react differently some are extremely claustrophobic and panic, scream, cry and even hyperventilate. Many are just distressed but are ok when someone shouts that help is on its way. Some are very calm even have a laugh. They are comfortable by pressing the emergency alarm button within the lift cage knowing that help will be summoned.

One Saturday morning we were called to our local community hospital for one female person shut in a lift. I was at the doors with Stoney who was OIC on this occasion. I shouted to the women that the fire service was now here and she would soon be released. Sometimes you can have a laugh with the lift occupants (if appropriate to do so. Not when they are in a blind panic) this lady was very calm. The reply from this woman was "Is that Tony?" I knew her, a woman called Carol who worked there and who I had known for a while. "Hi Carol yeah, it's Tone." Time to 'put her at ease' with a verbal prank that some have used before.

"Carol listen, we're going to get you out as soon as possible ok?" I said. "OK Tone", she replied.

I continue "It'll be around Wednesday Ok!?"

The response from Carol aimed at me was obviously deserved. She took this in good faith though. She had a good sense of humour. She was released within five minutes.

Some fire calls do sometimes need deciphering. A Saturday afternoon at around 3pm we were called to a Town called Bideford, approximately twenty miles from Ilfracombe. '022, 02C (ICV) - *BUILDING COLLAPSE ONE MALE REPORTED DECEASED – FIRE.'* We were backing up 041 and 042 (Bideford's pumps), 011 and 014 (one of

Barnstaple's pumps and the bronto) and the Urban Search & Rescue unit (USAR) from Exeter, East Devon. *"041 in attendance, 042 in attendance."* Both Bideford's pumps were now at scene but there sounded no immediate urgency in their voices. This shout seemed to end up a bit like a Chinese-whisper due to an over-panicked member of public who apparently knew the occupant of this building.

We were five miles from Ilfracombe when we heard instructions over the radio from our control *"014 stand-down return to station. 011- Return to home station. 022 return to home station. 02C return to home station, USAR return to home station."* "Eh? That's some building collapse that is!' I said sarcastically. 'I'll find out when we get back Jim Stone said through a smile.

"........Right ok thanks very much control. Speak to you soon, bye." Jim puts the phone down. "Well" he retorted with a sigh "This building collapse wasn't a building collapse at all! It was a MAN that had collapsed IN a building and died! He may have knocked something over which caused a small fire but which was out upon the Bideford's crew arrival." So there we have it. How things get misinterpreted. And our condolences to the chap involved.

It was 11pm on a cold November Saturday night. "021 & 022 - RTC- ROLLOVER." Sub officer Williams called out to the crews who were climbing aboard the pumps. A 'Rollover' is when a vehicle turns over either once or several times after an incident on the road. The vehicle can turn on its side then roof and repeat this action or uncommonly end over end. This can normally result in 'Pancaking' (flattening) of the A, B, C (D) posts causing a flattening of the roof trapping the occupant/s. I jumped aboard 021 and closed the door and we headed off to an area called Trimstone. When we arrived, followed closely by 022 with Sub O Derrin in charge, the Police were already in attendance. We dismounted from the pump and two of us followed Sub officer Williams a little way down a narrow lane to the single vehicle involved. As we approached we saw a BMW on its roof up against a high hedge, there was debris and scrapes in the road surface quite a way down the lane, pieces of hedgerow and bank were covering the road and stuck in the nearside wheel axles. The car was clearly pancaked resulting in a 'letterbox-type' slit between the doors, window sills and roof sills.

I was half expecting Ben to call for some extrication equipment to be set up but on noticing the fuel on the road he called back for a hosereel to be laid out. Ben, myself and another firefighter crouched down to peer inside the car with our torches expecting to see the occupant upside down as they weren't going to get out of this gap..............Nothing! With the torches we swept high and low and looked at each other across the upturned car in confirmation that there was no-one in the vehicle at all. I stood up stretched my back and noticed a Female Police officer walking across to us. "Any clues on where Houdini is?" I said as a joke still thinking that a person couldn't squeeze out of that gap.

She pointed down the road to a huddle of Officers by their Police cars. "Yes, One male occupant down there being breathalysed as we speak." I looked at her "Eh? One male occu........what, he climbed out of that?!" pointing to the sorry state of the BMW, "Did he turn to liquid first?!" She laughed and said that he was the driver and he did, somehow, actually squeeze out of the gap. I had a moment of removing my fire helmet and scratching my head at this job.

Ben asked if recovery was summoned which was organised by the Police as they may want the vehicle in situ first to carry out any investigations such as tyre pressures and skid measurements. He sent a message back to 022 that they could book available for an impending fire call whilst we witnessed the recovery, clear-up and wash down of the road. Then back to bed as a few of us was up early the next morning as some of us were representing the Fire Rescue Service in the annual Armistice parade.

Another memorable shout required the crew of 022 to respond to a 'car trapped' on the pier area 'below the chapel' one Saturday early evening. The chapel mentioned is St Nicholas's chapel on top of a very steep hill called Lantern hill as the chapel has a green flashing storm light on the roof for nautical purposes as this overlooks the Bristol Channel and the entrance to the local harbour. Two paths head up to the chapel from the base at the pier car park. One path wraps around the north side of the hill, the other wraps around the south side of the hill. The paths themselves are wide enough for people to walk up three or four abreast at points but narrows in places especially at the bottom of the south path. These are strictly for pedestrians only and not vehicles.

022 arrived and we all piled out looking around trying to be the first to spot the 'trapped car', with no success. I heard someone shout hello but couldn't see anyone. One of the boys went around the other side of the pump "Over here lads." We jogged round to his location and found him shielding the sun from his eyes pointing halfway up the south slope, and we saw.....a car facing downhill in a very tight spot!

The owner popped down to greet us "Hello Gents, seemed to have got myself into a spot of bother you see........."

Mick grabbed a rescue line and we all staggered up the hill, jumped onto the steep bank on the right and scrambled past the car to get behind it. The breeze hit us along with the unmistakable smell of burning clutch.

As is it transpired, the chap had seen the hill and thought he'd pay a visit to the top.....in his car. He managed to drive very slowly and extremely, if not painstakingly carefully, up to the top of the north path and down the south path only to realise that this path got narrower and increasingly tighter. He then decided to try and reverse very slowly back up the hill, as in the same mode as his north path ascent, in order to reverse back down the way he came. Only a few feet was gained at this slow pace until the clutch burned out and gave up. He wasn't sure who to call until his wife suggested 999 to see if we could help.

On assessing the situation the L/FF knew that there was no way of continuing downhill as a full wedge effect would take place, so as per original plan; we were going to have to pull the small car back up the very narrow hill (about 100 yards) and guide it back down the north path onto the pier. The OIC made pumps two for extra muscle whilst Mick attached one end of the line securely to the rear axle and made knots all the way up the line at intervals which enabled us to obtain a substantial grip. Whilst this was being done 021 was now at the pier with its crew making their way up to assist us. A firefighter got into the driver's seat and was ready to steer the car under the guidance of a firefighter behind and the cars mirrors.

With a countdown we all took the strain and held the car steady before all stepping backwards and moving the car uphill with just inches either side. This felt like it was beyond the traditional tug o' war.

With combined effort and excellent guidance and steering we managed to reach the apex of the hill. We then detached the line from the car and guided the reversing car back down the north side as there was no place to turn at the top, it was that tight.

The owner called recovery (for the car not us) and even though he was a little embarrassed all ended well.

One Wednesday evening at 7pm we attended a call to the harbour area of the town not far from the local lifeboat station.

'022 – person trapped – Ilfracombe harbour' (cove).

On-route we asked our control if they had any more information as regards to this entrapment, to which their reply was that a female was trapped three-quarters of the way up a tall ladder, lower limbs trapped and was in pain. I could only imagine her slipping off the ladder's rung but couldn't quite understand how she actually became trapped on a ladder. Carl nudged me "probably not trapped at all, just scared of heights and frozen on the thing."

We booked in attendance and similar to the last shout we could see no casualty initially. A woman came running over to us. "Hiya guys, down there" and pointed to the edge of the harbour wall. Still no casualty but then the edge of the wall started talking to us. "Hello, yes down here, quick." We peered over the wall to confirm this young woman's predicament.

The ladder in question was a vertical ladder which comprised of double rungs; so this particular ladder had two rungs adjacent each other with an approximate eight inch gap between the double rungs. This ladder was also known sometimes as a raking ladder. The ladder is bolted to the harbour wall so people can access their boats or return to the top when the tide is in. The casualty and the woman who alerted us, apparently the mother of the casualty was having a stroll along the beach, taking advantage of the ebbing tide, they decided to climb the ladder to reach the car park on the cove above the beach; she had climbed the ladder (wearing flip-flops) and as she neared the top her flimsy footwear slipped off, her leg slipped between the two rungs which wedged the limb tightly against both the metal bars in a vice-like grip; trapping her leg, just above the knee which was accompanied by ensuing pain. Craig Long the OIC came over to us. "We'll get the combi-tool spreaders connected and we'll force the rungs away from the limb. Bags, can you do the honours?" I gave him the nod "No problem mate." I then went over to the cove edge whilst the others were gathering the rescue equipment and rigging it for me. I laid down on the tarmac, popped my head over the side to assess the situation once more. "It hurts." The woman said with a concerned look. "I know love, it will hurt unfortunately. Listen, we are getting a spreading tool ready. I am going to position the tips of the spreaders between the two rungs and gently shift the metalwork out of the way ok?" She nodded her appreciation of the prospect of freedom. Her other leg was free and supporting her on the next rung down, she also locked her arm over the rung in front of her, so she would be safe when I freed her. Distraction worked well. "Well, you've picked a great spot here haven't you, with the panoramic view over the harbour AND you've attracted a crowd, fame at last eh?" She giggled as she looked at the onlookers. "Stop it, it's embarrassing." She cringed.

A tap on my shoulder indicated that the weber (pronounced *vaeber*) tool was ready, the 'Jaws of life' which we had previously used in RTC's, was the predecessor to this tool. Craig knelt next to me. "Is the reach ok Bags? Not too far down is it." I grabbed the spreaders, "No mate, fortunately she's near the top, and I can reach down easily to get the tool in place." The generator was started and I lowered the tool over the side. "What you going to do cut my leg off." The woman joked. "Nope, I'm going to squeeze it off! It's a spreader not a cutter. You ok?" she nodded and held on tightly to the rungs. I opened the spreader slowly as the tips could take purchase between the offending rungs, I placed the tension on slightly to avoid slippage then applied more pressure to slowly open the jaws which were close to her leg. Craig was looking at the whole ladder to check that the anchoring points were stable with no movement. I relocated the rungs two inches clear of the trapped limb which was sufficient enough for the casualty to move her leg; the rest of the ladder remained stable. Craig positioned a wooden wedge next to the spreader's tips so that it would assure no retraction against her leg when I closed the spreaders to remove them. I could now see a tight mark and bruising to the woman's thigh and discolouration above it with a paler colour to the lower part of her leg to her foot. She started to eagerly move as she was now free.

I held my hand out "Whoa, wait there for a second, let me move the tool out of the way and wait for the circulation to return to your leg. I placed the tool to the side of me and noticed an ambulance now in attendance. "It feels ok now, I've got sensation back." The woman said eagerly. "Ok then, up you come, nice and slowly though, we'll get the paramedics to check you over." She half climbed, half pulled herself up and off the ladder and as she limped I assisted her the few steps to the ambulance. Craig retrieved the wooden wedge and the crowd started to disperse. Craig then mentioned to the local authorities of what we had done to the ladder in order to remove the casualty so they could give the ladder a thorough check. The paramedics released the casualty from their care with advice only. She gave us a wave and said her thankyou's and was once again reunited with her flip-flop which was recovered from the beach below.

Both pumps were called to a gas leak late one evening to a property in town which housed three flats. The nature of this call was a 'smell of gas, potential gas leak'. Upon our arrival we couldn't smell gas externally but needed to investigate. A street lamp partially lit up the hall to this property but there was no movement within, no one came to greet us to say that they had made the call. One of the lads check the first floor flat by climbing the scaffold that was around the building and peering through the windows, no occupants visible. A smell of gas was now evident outside the main front door.

As the L/FF was about to knock on the main door he saw movement through the glass which he worked out was an elderly lady shuffling down the partially lit corridor. He shouted through the door "Hello love, it's the Fire Brigade. You may have a gas leak, we need you to come outside." He saw that the lady had her right arm up feeling her way down the hall using the wall as guidance but her hand was also heading for, what looked like, a light switch. "Don't switch the light on love, LEAVE IT!" the L/FF desperately shouted through the glass. The rest of us heard this alarming order, looked at the door then took cover. The L/FF was also ready to retreat round the corner of the building. The lady was very near the switch now as the L/FF shouted his instruction again. The elderly lady continued obliviously, "Hang on a minute dear I'll just turn the light on so I can see what I'm doing." This all happened in a matter of seconds. CLICK.....

The L/FF was still shouting out NOOOOO! When he very rapidly moved to the side of the building as the light switch was pressed. It was like slow motion, hearts in mouths.

Then.............Nothing. "What was you saying?" the lady casually asked. The L/FF sheepishly came back into view and said through, the now opened, door exposing the strong smell of gas. "I was saying that you may have a gas leak within this building and you need to get out. We didn't want you to turn your light on. Any others in this building, do you know?" The lady then realised the seriousness, or so we thought. "Oh, a gas leak I thought I could smell something. You didn't want me to turn on the light? Oh hang on then."

She turned round and walked to the door and raised her arm. "I'll turn it off again for you shall I?" Another CLICK whilst the majority of the crews were shouting NOOOOOOO! And taking cover once more. But still nothing. What a job!

The L/FF guided the lady outside and sat her on the fire engine. The remainder of us investigated the smell of gas which was traced to a gas hob left on in the ground floor flat. The occupant was present as he fumbled for the door in the dark after he listened to our warnings from the hall.

MESSING ABOUT!

One night we carried out an RTC drill where I was acting as the casualty with neck pain. The crew had an oxygen mask on me but no head support. "What are you playing at?" I said. "Support my head" Two of the firefighters then proceed to cheer my head in football match fashion "Baggy's head (clap clap clap. Baggy's head" (clap clap clap). A classic funny was when we drilled again with the Hughes Ejector pump. At a 90 degree angle to the rear of the appliance bay doors, there was an open-topped recess between the rear of the station and the workshop/BA compressor room/gym. This recess could accommodate one van or car if the car parking spaces were full. Two of our retained firefighters, local builders, drove into the station yard on that summers evening, windows down to make the most of the cool breeze before the drill session ahead and parked their van nose first in the recess space next to the workshop area. We kitted up and awaited our drill details. Leading firefighter McGovern suggested a combination drill using the 1.0.5 ladder to the roof of the gym and a 45mm hose carried aloft and got to work from that position. This was supplied by the pump; supplemented by the hydrant. Two firefighters where to control the branch on the roof, directing the jet over the left side of the building." We all acknowledged the drill detail. "Crews get to work." I was part of the ladder crew and two lengths of hard suction hose attached. Whilst we filled the dam up from the hydrant two firefighters had ascended the 105 ladder and was poised for the jet. So it was water on and the branch-men were happily directing the jet across the flat roof. A firefighter then came around from the recess side of the workshop looking concerned and went to speak to the Leading firefighter. "KNOCK-OFF- KNOCK-OFF!" Steve shouted. The pump revolutions were dropped immediately, and the hose shut. A few went over to the recess to see what the fuss was about. I thought that someone had left the rear door open and some water had entered the station. No, the water from the jet that merrily skimmed across the roof fell off the felt lip of the roof's edge, clipping the guttering and flying off into the open driver's window of the builder's van rapidly soaking the seats and interior.

The odd water fight, which is frowned upon now, used to go down well and these would be instigated by the slightest little thing. We once had both vehicles back on the forecourt at the front of the station after returning from a fire call. The pumps needed washing down so we would put the power take off in and give them a quick soap and wash off with the hosereels. A Firefighter offered up some water toward the other crew and Leading firefighter Stone sprayed back in retaliation. The firefighter then shot back a few more, well aimed, blasts over to the Leading firefighter. Stoney then fired back with a longer blast.

Before we knew it all four hosereels were off and got to work in a full water fight at the front of the station. Sub officer Derrin jumped off the pump "Right ok, that's enough. That'll do!" this statement temporarily fell on deaf ears as the water fight was now in full swing. He then stood between both pumps telling us to stop. "FOR CHRISTS SAKE THAT'S ENOUGH!" We scaled down the water fight and looked over to terry, he had a sly knowing smile, shaking his head as he stormed off past us into the station. "Bloody kids." He said as he disappeared, but took it in good light.

A Tuesday water fight after a summer's evening drill session led to an over keen use of water. All four hosereels were going well and a couple of the lads even stretched to using the station yard's static wall-mounted hosereel and even caught people out with buckets of water from the top of the appliances. Then we heard a massive blast of water hitting the ground at close proximity, we turned to see one of the lads struggling round the back of the pump with a fully charged 45mm hose heaving it toward us has he blasted away! "Not the jet Paul!" Jack shouted as we all dispersed to the far flung areas of the drill yard or to relevant safety of the appliance bay. The Sub let us have a little longer playing that time but when he saw the 45mm delivery hose in use he ordered a rapid 'knock-off make-up.' Which was immediately obeyed. Mocking the 'wet-behind-the-ears' probies was always good fun.

Several times some of the blokes used to set up tasks for them such as checking the reflectivity of the reflective strips that are stitched into the Hi-viz yellow RTC jackets by getting the probationers to shine a torch directly onto the strip for ten minutes to 'test it'! Or we would catch them out by getting them to ascend a ladder to the second floor of the drill tower and while they were up there the ladder crew would take the head of the ladder away from the building and lower it away from the second floor, by this time a couple of jets will be aimed at the two unfortunate probationers, up at the second floor, after the 'water on' command they would be blasted by the cold water from the jets. There was no escape, as the tower was constructed out of galvanised lattice beams and grills, so even a jet could be fired up the underside of the floor. We didn't 'punish' them for that long, maybe a ten second blast to acquaint them with water. Job done. We used to teach them that we could use the short extension ladder as a make-shift stretcher. We would obviously demonstrate this in front of the 'newbies' then get one of them to lay on the ladder to experience the pampering. With the probationer lying on the ladder we would have to tie him or her securely with a line by locking the feet in first then using half-hitches up the body and tying off the line on the round above their head. This was in case we would have to lower them from above or lifted from down below. Whilst the probationer was secured we would demonstrate that we could stand the ladder upright and they wouldn't slip out, then we would quickly flip the ladder over so that the probie was facing the ground to demonstrate that they would not fall out from this position either.

They never expected to be suddenly flipped over. We would then, cunningly, stand them back up to the vertical position, tie the ladder to the tower and give them a 'wash off' with the hosereel........again.

Another evening we had pump drills again. We were training off-station and proceed to one of the locations where we could 'lift' and pump water. We were at the junction of two roads. In the middle of the pavement was an inspection cover which; below this a culvert which transports water from a brook down to the sea at Wildersmouth beach. On the wall of this culvert below ground level there were two large planks of wood which were always hung up on hooks.

Accompanying these were two slots cut out in both walls opposite to each other. The planks slotted into these slots, one on top of the other, to make a temporary wall. A heavy duty salvage sheet was then placed over the top of the planks and weighted down. The water flowing down through the culvert built up to a sufficient depth as so we could introduce the hard suction hose into the water in order to lift it up and out into the receiving pump. The holes at the end of the strainer, where the water was entrained, must always be covered by water this is because if these holes were uncovered air would be entrained into the hard suction instead and the vacuum would be lost and so losing the lift up through the hose. All health and safety considerations were strictly adhered to as regards to the public and Fire service whether a fire and rescue incident or exercise. Warning lights and signs; indicating the hazards in the area were present throughout the exercise. To gain entry down into the culvert we placed a short extension ladder down the hole to gain access and egress, this allowed two firefighters to squeeze down (just about) and start boarding up and positioning the hard suction hose in the cramped space. Now, to the unsuspecting firefighter, normally the probationary firefighter, they would not notice a drain grid above their heads just behind them, or if they did; would not think twice about it. Why should they? But after a cruel prank by the firefighters on the jet above ground they would think twice about going down that hole and setting up again!

The set up - Two Probies descend into the hole, set up the water block, set up the hard suction and indicated to the guys above when all was ready to go, they remained down in the culvert to keep an eye on the strainer and water level. The pump operator lifts the water and delivers to the branchmen who then aimed the jet of water into the empty coach park opposite, or along the gutter, or................... directly down the drain back down onto the unsuspecting firefighters below in the culvert! It was not until they felt that their shoulders, back and neck felt the icy cold drench of intrusion that they realised that they were being blasted from their 'mates' above Always a cracking drill.

I must add, that like in any job, even though we did have a laugh and pull the odd prank, it was in no way detrimental to the health of any persons involved and did not interfere with the knowledge that needed to be gained by these drill. We all learned a tremendous amount and honed our skills immensely.

Another exercise which used to take place took place under our local swimming baths. This was in the form of a BA exercise. We would receive a brief back at the fire station and both pumps would set out and gather at the pool's pump/plant room entrance. The swimming pool was 25 metres in length and below this was a service tunnel that run the full length, it was a little awkward to access in BA as we had to negotiate pipes in the plant room to find a vertical ladder which led down ten feet into a pit, at one end of the pit at right angles was a square hole in the wall two feet from the ground, if you looked into thus hole and lit the area up with a torch then you would witness the 25 metre tunnel. We would climb up into this tunnel and could just about get through it either by extreme crouching or sliding on our fronts, we also shared this tunnel with several various-sized pipes which had the job of heating the large pool above. Several side pillars along the tunnel were a pain at times. Now, one more ingredient to this claustrophobic area was the heat. It was extremely hot down there exacerbated by our fire kit and cumbersome BA. So overall, ideal practice session. The exercises were usually devised by Sub O Derrin. He would set up the tunnel with casualty dummies and sometimes partial tunnel collapses half way through the tunnel where we had to remove the debris of rubble and shore up the collapse before locating the casualties and effecting rescues. It was very awkward to assess a casualty and place oxygen on them in a cramped space, then there was removing them by literally dragging them along on our knees whilst shuffling back bit by bit in the intense heat. When we emerged from the tunnel we had to drag the casualty a bit further to the vertical ladder where a line was passed down; we then used it to fashion a bowline in order to place around the casualty to be lifted out of the pit and into the plant room. By the time we took our BA and fire kit off we wouldn't have been no wetter if we went into the pool itself! It was a tough exercise, but I secretly enjoyed it.

NIGHT SHOUT – RETURNING TO OLD 'CLIFFE'

L ate one Saturday evening and we're back again to the derelict Cliffe Hydro hotel. 11.30pm the call came in of '*Smoke issuing*'. Due to the number of calls, indicating that this wasn't a false fire call, fire control ordered another two appliances to the scene, these were 161 from Woolacombe and 071 from combe martin. Both 021 and 022 turned up. The ground floor was boarded up accompanied with the front of the building surrounded by metal temporary fencing. Black smoke was issuing from large broken first floor windows, spiralling up into the night sky and around the glow of the street lamps. A couple of us were tasked to go around the exterior of the building, particularly the rear to see if there was any easy ground floor access and check for fire spread. The rear had been heavily secured and the few upper broken windows were emitting slight smoke and no flame evident at the time. As we radioed our observations back to Ben we walked back round to the front and saw more blue-lights from the additional appliances that had now arrived, we were met with another station's crew, one of their firefighters was using a large axe to cut through the many layers of plyboard which had been screwed to one of the front doors. The firefighter was doing really well but we doubted that he would give anyone else a go; as when he created a hole in the last layer the muscles and grip seemed to have seeped away and one last lob saw the axe had completed the final hole then the axe went flying out of the firefighter's hand, spun through the hole and ended up in the smoke-logged hallway. They used other wrecking tools to rip the remainder of the stubborn wood from the doorway. The main front door was now opened to expose the once glamorous lobby and the main staircase beyond. The Sub officer advised a defensive fire-fight as inside the floors were extremely damaged and dangerous as was some of the main structure. Ben ordered a 45mm jet to be got to work on a flickering glow menacingly teasing us just around the ascending 45 degree bend of the stairs which wrapped its way round an old elevator shaft leading to the first floor. Leading firefighter Stone organised a jet to accompany the hosereel that was earlier laid out and two firefighters trained the cold jet to the rear of the first floor stairs to rebound water off the walls to extinguish the fire that was probably rubbish around the back of the elevator shaft. Flames seemed to die down, smoke slowly dissipated and the OIC scaled the scene back down to two pumps. We made up the kit, another check through the door, replaced the fencing and jumped back on the pumps. As Ben passed his message back to our control a firefighter who was sat in the BA 1 position on 021 looked back out from the fire engine to the derelict structure. He stared for a moment then craned his head forward to focus on the upper floors. "Ben? Have a look at that. It's going again, look smoke's issuing from the first floor. Or am I seeing things?" We all looked on. Ben studied the windows. "Well. Yeah, you may have a point, hang on."

He then swung the dashboard address light around to fix the beam on the first floors. "Yeah it is Ben it's going again!" says the

Leading firefighter. The Sub agreed. "Right boys, get a hosereel off, get the fencing out of the way and check the main lobby area again."

This was proving a stubborn little fire this one. However there may have been another fire or a rekindling of the first which was probably the case due to the spaces and voids throughout the building entraining air flow. I assisted with the fencing then grabbed the hosereel branch from the pump operator from above the pavement railings. I could see some smoke but no flame.

Another firefighter and myself were given the all clear to proceed into the large derelict dining room to the left to check for fire, we found none. As we came back out I noticed that annoying flickering behind the lift shaft again. I stayed where I was and opened the hosereel jet and aimed it at the top of the stairs. The fire ceased but I waited and watched cunningly to catch it out. I could hear bits of old plaster dropping around us from being loosened from the dousing earlier. I edged forward for a closer look. "Go careful Bags, not too far mate, it's unstable in there." Ben called out with concern. I looked back with the thumbs up and noticed Ben and Stoney stood a little way into the lobby. "Shit, it's started up again." I said as I witnessed the flames. "I need the small tools; I can see the fire now. It's behind the lift shaft under the stairs." I could clearly see the orange flickering through the bare cracked stairs. "I'll just need a jemmy (Small crowbar)." I returned to the lobby entrance area where Stoney handed me the jemmy bar. I walked back to the stairs and slowly ascended a step at a time. Using the stronger part of the staircase close to the wall armed with my tools I climbed four stairs and CRACK, CREAK and a sound of splintered wood falling into the basement area. I stopped momentarily then ascend again.

"Bloody hell go steady bags" Stoney called out.

"Alright mate nearly there," I called back without looking at him. I reached the upper stairs on the bend behind the lift-shaft. Sounds of cracking and creaking were still evident as I started to dig into a gap between the stair tread and riser; and prised the wood apart. For old wood it was very stubborn but I destroyed the remainder to gain good access to the fire. The smoke was virtually nil as the large draughts from the openings at the front were blowing the smoke up the staircase to the upper floors. The sweet pungent smell of smoke was still intruding the nasal passages all the same. A large gap was now created; I could see the fire merrily burning away. *'Such a menial fire causing all this trouble'*. I gave the fire a good drink with the hosereel and checked thoroughly to satisfy myself that it was completely extinguished. I backed slowly down the stairs as my foot sunk into a rotten tread resulting in more falling material. "Come on Baggy, let's go mate." The Leading firefighter called. "I wasn't planning in staying any longer. Let's sod off." We secured and monitored the building - success. Fire out.

A STRANGE ROAD
TRAFFIC INCIDENT

'C omyn Road' is a B-road which runs from Ilfracombe to Barnstaple, Just outside of central Ilfracombe the road runs alongside a Holiday complex and a local sports field. Between these two landmarks is to be the setting for our next incident.

Both 021 and 022 along with an Ambulance made our way to this location one Sunday morning at 11.20am, as we received reports of a two-car RTC, Persons trapped. As we approached the scene I could feel the pump slow down. I looked up from the rear of the cab whilst I was getting my kit on, and saw two cars in a front quarter oblique collision approximately one hundred metres up the road before a right-hand bend. Our driver was taking in what was going on immediately in front of the pump. "Look at this lot!" he said in disbelief. I craned my neck to get a look onto the road below us to witness seven young people laying randomly all across the road metres away from the two vehicles. Had they been struck by one of the vehicles? "It looks like something on a film set." I quipped. These people were actually in the cars minutes before. We jumped out and checked a few of these youngsters who didn't really have anything wrong with them, not even shock. We got them to the side of the road. Sub officer Derrin got onto the radio and asked for the urgent attendance from the Police as the cars ahead had completely blocked the road. Some of the young people said that they had suffered back pain, they were on the pavement so at least we could leave them in situ and in the care of the Ambulance crew who were also now in attendance and requesting more Ambulances. "Why are you all lying down on the road?" one of the firefighters asked the group, which had just got up with minor injuries. "Oh, a bloke saw us get out of the car and told us to lie down and keep still, where we were." Strange, I could understand if they all had C-Spine/ back pain. The OIC asked if anyone was still in the cars, which were at a 90 degree angle to each other. We were informed that someone was still in one of the cars, a Ford Sierra; this had collided with a small Volkswagen car. Our crew mounted the appliance and drove a little way to the vehicles. I stepped of the pump and peered in to find a young lad in the driver's seat in pain he had facial injuries and he was physically trapped. Terry told us to start getting the RTC kit off and to set up an equipment area; he checked the other car before returning to the young driver who was conscious and breathing throughout the rescue. We set the kit up, and liaised with the Ambulance service as regards to how they would like us to extricate this guy. We informed them that he was trapped by the legs and now seemed to be in and out of consciousness. They thought the same as us and opted for a full roof removal as this lad was complaining of back and neck pain, he also sustained leg, chest and head injuries. I heard another firefighter say that there was no-one in the other vehicle and the occupants were probably the people that were lying on the road. We started to remove the roof after removing the glass that at least was intact in the frames.

Some of the other firefighters were making the vehicle safe such as washing down some fuel and absorbing oil and sweeping clear broken glass that was shattered across road.

The roof came off swiftly and safely. We then rotated the tools to others once more and started to push away the metal from around the casualty's legs by utilising a 'dashboard roll' this is basically pushing forward the bulkhead away from the legs thus freeing them. Word came about that one of the casualties, a young lad, from one of the cars was missing; he was not with the group we spoke to. This statement resulted in much confusion. I looked around and couldn't see anyone fitting the description within the immediate vicinity; the Police had now turned up and started to look for this missing person. I looked up at the high bank from the Holiday complex to witness lots of holiday-makers getting quite an open aerial view of the rescue extrication in progress.

The casualty was starting to moan and groan in pain at this point, Paramedics who had gave him Entonox gas was now sat next to him to attempt to insert a cannula into his arm to administer the stronger analgesic, morphine. In order to keep the casualty's dignity intact we had a couple of spare guys, that weren't immediately involved in extrication work, to set up some large salvage sheets over the back of the car and suspend them in place as to screen the scene off from the crowd above. Once these were in place we could hear from high up behind the 'screens' comments like "Oh they've put screens up, that's not a good sign" or "Oh poor chap he must have 'gone' now" These assumptions were annoying the crews, one of the firefighter's actually popped his head around the salvage sheets and waved the people away "Go on, go away." he said whilst trying to wear a friendly smile. Me and that firefighter was not carrying out any immediate rescue work as we had not long assisted in the roof removal and other firefighters had taken over the Dash-roll. We were tasked to have a look around in the nearby sports field and holiday complex behind us.

As we searched I joked that the only guy that fitted the description that we was given was the lad in the car! We meet up with the Police officers who told us that they had no luck at that point, they had searched around the chalets, me and the other firefighter searched the other side of the complex such as the shop, bar, pool area and talked to staff but found nothing. Our radio alerted us to one of the Leading firefighters who called us back to the scene. "Yeah, come back lads this person has been found." As we got back to the scene I asked the whereabouts of this missing person. The Leading firefighter pointed to the now partially trapped driver "There he is!" I looked at the Leading firefighter. "What a weird shout this has turned out to be." It was like I had to pinch myself to escape a weird dream. One of the casualties down the road apparently was confused and said that this lad was missing unaware that he was literally attached to his car as he was trapped and could not join them. We made sure that the removed windscreen and various lightweight materials was either lashed down or placed underneath the car as we were told by the Paramedics that the Devon Air Ambulance was on its way in.

The Police was dealing with the landing area. Within two minutes I heard what sounded like two helicopters approaching. I didn't see where they had landed but presumed the obvious site was that of the sports field near the scene. Some firefighters were helping ambulance crews carry the injured up to the field, so this confirmed my thoughts on the chopper's landing area. Other casualties were being loaded into land ambulances. We were then informed that the trapped casualty was also going to hospital by air. Now free, the casualty was gently transferred onto a longboard, he was still drifting in and out of consciousness. The Paramedics were constantly monitoring the lad's pulse and breathing rate. We all assisted the paramedics in carrying the casualty into the sports field. Two helicopters had landed with rotor blades still frantically and menacingly spinning. We were ushered over to the Devon Air Ambulance where our casualty was carefully placed and secured whilst the air crew took over the care of him. The others were on board a large yellow Search and Rescue Sea-King helicopter from nearby Royal Marines Barracks at Chivenor. The Police investigated the scene in which they had found that the sierra had more than likely skidded on an area of diesel that had been spilt on the highway causing the collision. All involved made a good recovery.

DOC 'SPOCK'

10pm one warm summer's Thursday evening. '022- *Person locked out of flat.'* 022 turned up to the block of flats not far from the station and we're met by Dr Spock Minus the Starship Enterprise! He was stood on the pavement awaiting our arrival dressed in black boots, black trousers, and purple shirt with the Startrek logo emblazoned upon it and to top it all to express the correct attire, the pointy ears. Leading firefighter McGovern was OIC and stepped off the pump to greet the guy "Ah, Mr Spock, did you beam us up?" The 'Doctor' nodded "yes, I've locked myself out of my flat and my medication is inside which I need to take urgently. I live on the second floor at the side of this place" he said pointing to the building. "I have a small window open, up there." he pointed again at the window. That's half the battle anyway, I thought. The Leading firefighter turned to us "Right lads we'll have the 1.0.5 ladder off and pitch to the second floor window." As we pitched the ladder one of the lads chatted to 'Spock'. "So you're a 'Trekkie' then are you?" He looked surprised. "Well actually I'm a 'Trekker' that's the proper terminology." The firefighter nodded in acknowledgment then looked across at the rest of us with a 'Whatever' look on his face. "Could I have my medication and keys brought down please as I am going to visit a friend in Town?" The TREKKER asked. One of the blokes ascended the ladder, gained access, grabbed the guy's medication and keys, secured the flat and descended by a more normal means via the internal stairs. "Where you been then mate? Fancy dress party or something like that?" one of the lads pries. "No, I have been to a Trekkers convention. We meet up every year." Leading firefighter McGovern talked to him as we placed the ladder back onto the pump. "Where are you off to now then?" "Oh, I'm going to the high street to meet a mate of mine." Stevie smiled. "Want a lift to the high street? We're going that way." The Trekker looked overwhelmed "Oh that'd be really great! Thank you so much. Thank you, that'll be brilliant!" We all found this emotional excitement amusing. *'A star trek convention AND a ride in a fire engine! Who'd have thought eh?!'* I said to no one in particular. Anyway, 'Spock' squeezed in with us lot in the back I did suggest that he sat on the Leading firefighter's lap up front. (He never did). We dropped 'spock' off at the high street in all his regalia and we beeped and waved like mad to the locally-famed fella and headed back to station.

During the next week after returning from a shout, we rounded a corner from the sea front to the high street and who did we see? Dr Spock again (In normal civilian attire). "There's SPOCK someone shouted, we all looked out of then cab and spotted him. The driver blasted the horn a couple of times and we all waved and stuck our thumbs up. He waved and smiled back and as we passed and he continued walking through the shoppers he had a look of either appreciation or embarrassment. Probably the latter.

ROAD TRAFFIC COLLISIONS

At around 10pm one Wednesday evening both pumps were called to an RTC in town, just a few of metres from outside where we had the roof alight. Sub officer Derrin was in charge of 021; 022 followed swiftly with leading firefighter McGovern in charge. Police were already at the scene. As we approached we saw one large family-sized car on all four wheels in the middle of the road at an angle. A police officer walked over to Terry and gave him the details of what he thought had happened. "Abandoned RTC, looks like the car had been tanking down this road, lost it a bit and hit the parked car over there." he pointed to a blue car with a smashed offside. "They've then stopped, or the car's deflected and stopped more like, and whoever was driving has done a runner probably, nobody about." I looked over at the car involved that was now steaming from under the bonnet and walked over to it with a couple of the lads to get the bonnet open to check for fire and to make safe. There was quite a lot of frontal damage. Terry finished his conversation with the officer and called for a few of the lads "Listen in then, we think that the occupant/s may have done a runner but to err on the side of caution let's get a good look around the area in case someone has been injured, dazed and wandered off". So we went searching the area to no avail. We left the scene in the hands of the Police and headed back to station once the car was made safe.

A couple of nights later both pumps were called to a steep road, off the sea front, to another RTC. We turned up to see a small Mini car on its side halfway up this road. The roof facing us as we approached from the bottom of the road. Sub officer Williams was OIC. He radioed the pump driver. "Could you put an informative message back (to control) Road Traffic Collision, involving one car on public highway. No persons trapped, no persons present. Police required." Ben looked around. "Ok boys a quick look around, we'll await the Police. Can we have a couple of you to get a hosereel off and wash down the fluid from the car?" By the time we had a look about and washed the road down the Police were in attendance. I looked around the car and said to my mate "How the bloody hell can someone get a car on its side on a steep hill like this and not turn it on its roof? The car's roof looked unscratched and no deformation to the structure as if it had rolled or skidded right down the road hitting the wall, nothing of the sort. "Must have all been in slow motion." He laughed. We wasn't sure that the handbrake was applied, so we couldn't push it back on all four wheels as it may have rolled forward striking the crews and other vehicles. A recovery vehicle could manoeuvre the car first and restrain it from moving once upright.

The Police awaited vehicle recovery and carried out various checks via their Police National Computer database and we left the scene of another abandoned RTC. At least they were lucky enough to be able to extract themselves to abandon the vehicles safely.

At six forty five in the morning on a crisp Wednesday morning both pumps were called to a small area called Watermouth. We had received a report of an RTC involving two vehicles and it mentioned 'persons trapped'. It did not take long to drive through down and out to Watermouth as it was early in the morning and hardly any traffic on the road.

Upon our arrival we found that the road was completely blocked, so Terry asked control if the police had been called as well as the ambulance service. Confirmation came back that the ambulance was on-route and the police had been called. The collision was between a large transit van and a low sports-styled car. The impact was an offside (driver to driver) front quarter oblique impact with massive twisting distortion to both vehicles. The car's engine compartment had be pushed back into the bulkhead and resulted in an intrusion involving the dashboard and steering wheel which, in turn, trapped and fractured the young male casualty's legs. He received arm, chest and head injuries too, but was conscious and breathing, so he was scrutinised constantly checking on his vital signs and breathing. This was advanced when the ambulance crew took over from us. In the van no persons were trapped, the driver escaped the wreckage with minor injuries. An equipment area was established, lighting set up and hydraulic rescue tools connected to the generator. Others were dealing with the trapped casualty, placing an oxygen mask on his face to keep his cell tissues perfused. The car was very quickly stabilised and was made as safe as possible. A hosereel was laid out in case of spillage or fire. The van was winched back several feet and the firefighters were all around the car removing the glass (the glass which was actually still intact) and removing the rubber door seals and plastic trim.

The ambulance crew were now on-scene and immediately assessed the casualty and asked Terry how long would it take to remove the whole roof. They were initially looking for a quick side entry removal but due to neck pain and the head impact and injury they erred on the side of caution; and requested the roof off. "It's all prepared mate, just say the word and the roof will be removed within a few minutes" the Sub told them. Some of the lads were already at the nearside A-post and the generator loudly protesting its early wake up call. The ambulance guy checked the casualty's vital sign's once more "he's stable, but needs to come out on the longboards over the seats when you've released him. Can we have the roof off?" Terry shouted over the noise of the generator "right guys, roof off please, now! The first cuts commenced along the nearside of the car, I checked stabilisation was all secure. As I stood up I noticed the 'jaws of life' cutters in the closed position next to me being held by a sweating firefighter.

"Want me to have a bash mate, rotate the tool and all that?" eager to get stuck in and start methodically severing through the offside posts. "Yeah, great, cheers bags. All yours." As he carefully passed the cutters across. I had cut the D, C and bottom of the B post and went to walk round the paramedic kneeling at the driver's door assessing the occupant. "Rest there Baggy." Terry said.

I paused and stepped back slightly, wiping my face and aware that the dawn was breaking offering some rays of sunlight through the dense trees on the banks of the road. "Neutralise green" I shouted over to jack who was on the generator in order the make the cutters safe. "The paramedic wants to do a quick assessment, so we'll let him do his stuff and get stuck in again." Terry nodded. I nodded back in acknowledgment. After about thirty seconds the paramedic had completed his assessment. "Righto Lads, that's great stuff. He's stable. Thanks guys." I moved in for my last cut to the bottom of the deformed offside A-post. "Energise green". I shouted over to jack and felt the vibration of the movement through the cables due to the rapid energy transfer. The other ambulance guy was fetching the stretcher, longboard and blocks from the ambulance. Behind me I could hear the others setting up the ram for a probable 'dashboard roll' manoeuvre. After I had severed the A-post Terry asked Craig to assist me with the complete removal of the front driver's door. This was swiftly carried out whilst the paramedic offered some room. The sub looked at the dashboard. "Alright Bags? Make a quick cut along the sill at the bottom of the A-post will you? Then go have a drink. We'll have to go for a dashboard roll." (I said we would didn't I?!) I made the snip in the sill then shouted over to jack to neutralise green whilst I moved well out of the way. Another casualty assessment by the ambulance guy and the others turn on the wrecked vehicle. I was thrown a bottled water (plastic) which connected with my fire helmet (thanks mate!) and guzzled it down whilst I heard the order of 'energise orange' and the ram slowly extended from the bottom of the B-post to, just below, the cut section of the A-post as my last cut along the sill ripped apart and widened. This was carried out under the blue sky of daylight now. A wedge was placed into the cut in the sill to keep it open and the ram repositioned for another push. Slowly but surely the offending dashboard and bulkhead was pushed away from the driver's legs; exposing some significant injuries and causing him even more discomfort. The paramedic drew up some more painkilling drug and administered it through a cannula in this guy's arm which was inserted early on in the job. I heard a voice from the rear of the car "Anyone spare? I need to stretch." It was Matt who had been holding the driver's head in neutral alignment for such a long time. I threw my empty bottle onto the pump and walked across but he was just swapping as I got there. "You alright Matt? Did we forget about you?" I said with a wry smile. "Sodding hell mate, I've seized up!" he said whilst shaking his arms and stretching his back. "Right everyone, around the car, we're going to assist in removing the casualty in a bit." We all gathered round the wreckage in which we had also now made into a convertible. The driver's seat's backrest was slowly lowered back after the longboard was slid down behind this poor chap.

Jim was now holding the driver's head so he called the shots. "Right listen in" he said, "It's only my voice you should be hearing unless the paramedics tell us otherwise. The order will be 2, 3 lift and we will slide the driver six inches up the board on 'lift' reposition an so on, ok?" "2, 3 LIFT." We all assisted in moving this guy on the board until he was tilted back and was horizontal over the seats.

The longboard straps were attached followed by the head-blocks, another check by the paramedics and removed him completely from the wreckage and onto the ambulance stretcher, then into the ambulance.

We remained a further twenty to thirty minutes sweeping and washing down the road of liquid and debris, whilst the police took tyre pressures and measurements. The occupant of the van suffered with shock and the occupant of the car had a few leg fractures, a fractured arm, broken ribs and facial injuries, and survived the collision.

WELL ALIGHT!

"H *OUSE FIRE – WEST DOWN-BOTH PUMPS."* The firefighter shouted the details from the call slip out to us. West down is a small village two miles to the south of Ilfracombe, a quaint little village with a village square. We were called to a house within the square near the village pub; which had reminded me that I needed to celebrate later as it was my birthday! We got the shout at 2.30pm and I was riding 022 and my BA team-mate was leading firefighter McGovern. We arrived at scene and there was obvious thick black smoke issuing from the right side first floor window of the property, billowing across the square. The first BA team had their brief and entered the property. We dismounted from 022 and headed for BA control. Sub officer Derrin was waiting. "Right meet up with the first team, who will be up on the first floor now, and take another hosereel up with you. It's the kiddie's room." As I was rigging my facemask I looked at the Sub. "Oh Christ, is it persons reported then?" he nodded. "No, we've had the all clear from the occupant, they're all accounted for. In you go." Steve and I made our way up the stairs and saw the lower legs of the first BA crew through the heavy smoke. "What's happening? The room's on the right!" I shouted. I could feel

the burning on my ears as we manoeuvred closer. We all knelt down as the first team checked the door with the back of the hand, and a spray-check on the door revealed steam very low down (as this was all we could see at the time). Team one then 'cracked' the door ajar. A roar of flame menacingly leapt out towards us then back again as if to lure us in. The team gave the flames a quick blast with the jet and shut the door to let it do its preliminary work. The next time they opened it we both bunched up and hit the fire back in unison. Smoke was now even thicker on the landing area. And the heat was intense that it was even stinging my face through the mask. The room was all consumed with fire, it was well alight. We knocked the fire back into the room, hit the ceiling to clear all the loose debris and extinguished the fire. I heard a very deep voice from the stairs "You alright lads?" The voice wasn't muffled as it would if wearing BA but very clear. I stepped out of the room onto the landing retracting our hosereel as I went and tried to see down the stairs from where the voice had come from; but obviously saw nothing due to the smoke at a low level. I'm joined by Steve and we started to descend the stairs as another crew passed both us and the first crew to relieve us and started dampening down. We needed a cool off and a drink as it was also a hot afternoon. "You alright lads?" the clear voice again, I bent down and came face to face with a pair of leggings, the other half of the body must be in the smoke layer! The voice was at the bottom of the stairs; and it belonged to Divisional Officer (DO) Price. "Come and have a breather boys." he said as he slowly materialised into a human form as he walked down the stairs out of the smoke. He looked at us all as we walked out into the fresh air toward BA Control. "Well done lads, good job."

The DO said with a smile then he went to talk to another officer. Back then I was a smoker (part-time), not what I called a regular every day smoker but after a couple of beers or a hefty job like this....

occasionally. It wasn't right to be seen in public smoking so we tried to find somewhere out of the way. Stevie McGovern called me over "C'mon Bags, we'll go over next to the pub in the walkway." The walkway was between the pub and a house. A few more of the lads joined us as we eagerly lit our ciggies knowing that we were not quite out of public sight. We were chatting and puffing away when one of the lads at the end of the alley spotted the DO heading towards us. "The D.O.'s coming!" We all put our ciggie-holding hands behind our backs and quickly blew out the half inhaled smoke to be carried away by the draught and continued to chat until we saw the DO walk past us smiling at us all. After various greetings from the firefighters, such as a nod accompanied with "Sir", "Alright Boss", "Hiya Sir," He acknowledged us and reached the end of the alley to enter the side door of the pub (which he was utilising as a control and interview point rather than alcoholic refreshment). We all looked at each other chuckling, close one. Then whilst we still had hands hidden, the DO turned round to us, still smiling "It's alright lads you can carry on smoking, I'm going to have a cigar myself." I thought AH, spotted, Oh well crack on. After our quick break we grabbed various small tools and ceiling hooks and proceed back up to the fire-damaged bedroom to take apart the ceiling, or the remainder of it at least, and pulled up burnt floorboards to look for and extinguish any remaining hotspots and to start the sweating process all over again. We confined the fire to the bedroom only and it had not spread anywhere else, apart from the obvious smoke damage. So this was a good stop. No injuries, everybody accounted for. The fire was under full Investigation by the fire service.

A few years later we were back at West Down again one Thursday evening at around 7pm.We were called to a large domestic garage on fire in the village square......next to the house that had the bedroom fire. Not linked at all though. As both pumps entered the square we saw large amounts of smoke around about the village square; then flames as we approached the garage. Leading firefighter Long was OIC on this job. We dragged a couple of hosereels off the appliances and a jet laid out which water was trained through the large gap in the now blackened garage door. As we knocked the flames back myself and some of the firefighters started using a large axes and sledgehammers on the buckled garage door to bend it slightly so we could get purchase on the edges to rip it away to gain access to the fire within. The garage was going well; but we immediately hit it with the jets. The Leading firefighter urgently came over to us. "Can you start hitting the left side of the garage? As the owner just mentioned that there are Calor gas cylinders in there on that side near the back." We couldn't see them due to the intensity of the fire and the smoke created by it. A couple of popping sounds were heard from within the fire, probably aerosols going off and paint tins.

Craig came over again and mentioned that there were three windows at the back which were emitting flames close to the other building that was backing onto the garage. I immediately grabbed a hosereel and pulled it round to the alleyway (where we had our ciggies on the last fire!) I got the hose to work at the rear windows to extinguish any fire that was present, also to cool any cylinders in that vicinity. To my left behind the garage was a small walkway, too narrow to risk firefighting from due to this narrow area as the flames were reaching across the gap, so I fought the fire at an angle from the alley.

In between the flames I looked over to the other end of the walkway to see if another firefighter was making the most of the wider area over that side using a jet from that end. I couldn't see any firefighters through the intermittent flames and smoke, but I did see someone else who was shimmering like a mirage through the heat. I had to squint as I could not believe what I was seeing. I witnessed a member of public near the far end of the walkway, quite close to the rear windows of the flaming, ticking-time bomb' of the garage dressed in T-shirt, shorts and flip-flops trying to shield himself from the intense heat whilst feebly attempting to extinguish the ferocious flames with......a garden hose. I mean, good on him for his community spirit and it's great that he'd thought that he'd have a go but this was extremely dangerous for the guy in flimsy summer clothing and cylinder heating up rapidly within the flames. This area was soon for evacuation. I shouted across at him "Oi MATE." Nothing. "Oi YOU!" He looked over at me. "GET BACK." He then nodded with a smile as he hadn't acknowledged what I said (or ignored me) and continued squirting a small limited-pressurised amount of water out of the garden hose as if he was doing us and the owner a favour. The spray from the domestic garden hose was evaporating into mist as it approached the building. I thought we were meant to be the daft ones by running into a fire whilst everyone else runs away from it! I risked stepping into the walkway and shouted even louder "Oi, YOU.GET BACK NOW! GO ON SOD OFF BACK!" He looked at me either shocked or confused in what I still wanted him to do; he then slowly walked away from the burning building back into a garden. "STAY BACK, WE'VE GOT THIS MATE OK? STAY IN ONE PIECE." I finalised my protest and got back to firefighting. He waved a hand at me in acknowledgement and fully retreated, I put my thumb up happy that he acknowledged and stepped back to safety. I wondered how the lads were getting on at the front. 051 from Braunton was now in attendance, I saw some of their crew rushing around then saw a blackened butane cylinder which had been pulled from the extinguished area from the front of the garage; the guys from Station 05 were cooling it with water spray and checking the temperature with a thermal imaging camera. I knocked back the fire in the first two windows nearest to me, and then reached across into the walkway to knock out the last bit of ferocious flame. I then stepped back into the alley and knocked the hosereel off in preparedness to return to the front of the garage in support of the guys there.

Then **BANG.** I forced myself back further into the alley and ducked my head; I felt something hard impacting with my fire helmet as I crouched down as I wasn't quite sure what damage the obvious explosion had done or what direction any debris was being thrown, even though I took an impact. I looked to the side of the garage in front of me which was now obscured by smoke. As the smoke cleared I saw a large crazy vertical crack in the side wall leaving the back end leaning out slightly and the other half leaning even further at approximately a twenty degree angle. I then looked down to see small chunks of masonry laying around me and in the pub car park. I realised that this damage was due to an undiscovered gas cylinder which had exploded through the heat of the fire. Leading firefighter Long came running around the corner in a matter of seconds looking concerned. "BAGS, BAGS YOU OK?!" "Yeah, I'm ok thanks mate. I'm finished back here I'll come round to the front now" I said as I dragged the hosereel round with me. Craig looked at me again and with an exasperated chuckle he nodded his head "PHEW shit mate that was something?" I rubbed the sweat from my face. "You're telling me, they say adrenaline is brown eh?" With the fire now extinguished we spent some time dampening down and cooling cylinders to reduce the risk of further explosions.

In the past we, as a team, we had rescued a fair few people from fire and RTCs over the thirteen years that I had served. A great sense of achievement; the feeling that you have helped someone when no one else can. Job satisfaction was, and is today I don't doubt, at the apex of priority and demand. I have taken part in rescues of a parrot (in its cage) and two guinea pigs (in their cage) at the same job, a house fire. Several persons rescued from the upper floors and flat roof at the rear of a block of flats whilst the building is on fire, intoxicated people who had fallen asleep and left food on the cooker smouldering away after a night out; shocked to be woken by a couple of firefighters assisting them out of the building when they were unaware of their predicament. Also a fire in a rear room of a care home in Ilfracombe one Saturday evening resulted in ten residents being rescued from the smoke-filled building, the fire was discovered to be an armchair that was well alight. Extricating crash victims to rescuing people shut in lifts.

Fire, in the wrong context, is a horrible and dangerous element. It cleanses everything in its path whilst producing noxious smoke that is made up of many poisonous chemicals. It is only a matter of seconds that a fire victim would be overcome by smoke inhalation in which the victim could succumb to, then could even be consumed by fire itself if not rescued. This obviously extends to animals too. I like animals, so it is sad to even see these succumb to fire and smoke.

One Monday morning we experienced a sad occasion when we attended a house fire in which there was smoke issuing from the whole of the first floor, as second crew we were tasked to go in for a search and rescue task.

The first crew entered the house to attack the fire with hosereels, a jet was run out due to the spread and intensity of fire, they made their way through to the rear of the property where the kitchen was, and where the fire was at its most concentrated and intense. We entered the house and checked the lounge on the left, we felt, with our boots, objects on the floor as we used the BA shuffle to sweep around. On tapping something with our boots we bent down to feel fur. two dogs were lying on the floor facing each other, nose to nose, obviously deceased, two cats also found in another room, dead, a parrot at the bottom of its cage, dead, a couple of hamsters in their cage in another room also succumbed to the exposure of the thick black choking smoke. Upstairs we continued to search, nothing else was found. We radioed to BACO as regards to the pets beyond help then headed back down the stairs to the kitchen area on the left side of the house to the rear. The crew inside were extinguishing the last of the flames and commenced in damping down, we assisted with the hosereel. The whole room was gutted beyond recognition to the fact that it ever *was* a kitchen; apart from the distorted cooker. The whole window unit had melted, burned and had fallen out of the building leaving a large black whole where it once was securely fixed in place. I carefully walked out into the attached utility room, which had also damaged by heat and smoke, to check for fire spread and hotspots. I walked outside and looked back at the exterior walls that once were brilliant white in contrast with the smart black glossed downpipes and guttering, the white walls were now scorched, deeply blackened in a display of ugliness of the evidence that fire was present and strong. The crews salvaged what they could and we all helped move most of the contents to open air. It was quite heart-breaking to carry out photo albums of which had been smoke damaged or even burnt; all these sentimental items that had been wiped out in a short space of time. This was a sad day for the occupants of this house and firefighters alike. The occupants were out at the time.

THINGS THAT GO BUMP.....
AT ANYTIME.

G as cylinders - the potential time-bomb when involved in fire. We attended a commercial address in Come Martin one Sunday morning; a workshop on fire. Several appliances attended due to the multiple calls from members of public. So we arrived, saw that a fire was rapidly developing inside the workshop, so we were ordered to don BA and enter the building to fight the fire which was located at the far end of the workshop. There were many items lying around, even with the BA shuffle procedure we were still caught out by random items at times. On entering another side room, which was similar to a domestic garage, we searched that area for any fire spread, there were some fire along the far wall which had broken through the partition, we quickly extinguished it and checked the rest of the 'annexe'-type Building. As the smoke was slowly venting from doors and windows so the smoke level was obviously rising whilst dissipating I spotted what looked like gas cylinders lined up. There were approximately six of them, one was Propane, three were butane and two were Oxy-acetylene cylinders (used in welding). They were located by the main garage door in this part of the building. My mate immediately informed BACO of the dangerous findings, who in turn informed the OIC; we then went back into the main workshop and informed other BA crews of the obvious danger. We withdrew and used a jet from the far end entrance of the workshop at the main doors to fight the fire; we fought it in defensive mode. A crew was called to force the lock on the far garage door in order to ventilate and cool the cylinders. Once the door was opened one of the firefighters used his touch to gauge the temperatures of the three cylinders nearest the door, they were cool as the fire had not yet touched them, however they could still be heated up from the temperature of the flames and free heat, so they had to be checked with a thermal imaging camera (tic). This device shows the presence (or not) of heat- blue being cold and red being hot. It produces a video picture like a negative. A few of us assisted with the removal of the butane and propane cylinders to an open area, checked for hotspots and witnessed a slight orange colouration on the *tic*; hosereels were immediately trained on these cylinders. Attention was now drawn to the oxy-acetylene cylinders. The two cylinders were standing on purpose-built wheeled trucks which enabled them to be wheeled about where they are needed. These were also cool to the touch but, these cylinders have an internal make up similar to a honeycomb insert which free-heats and has an exothermic effect which means that it keeps heating with the potential of exploding, unless cooled, usually for twenty four hours in a skip of water or a pool for example. These cylinders were then wheeled outside and we immediately got a jet onto them from a distance, even that they showed that they had not been heated significantly. We were taking some cover holding hand-branches cooling these things.

A Sub officer attached to Barnstaple station came over to us, had a look at all the cylinder through the tic then said "Lash the hoses fast lads and just let the water do its work. You all come away over here. You don't need to be near them, it's not bloody worth it!"

He was absolutely right, it was not worth being maimed or killed. We used either some lines off the pumps or personal lines to lash the hose to various items strewn around the yard. No explosions did occur, thankfully and the cylinders cooled down sufficiently after several hours.

A few years before I joined the Brigade, there was a fire on Barnstaple's patch; A fire in a motorcycle workshop. A very serious intense fire which resulted in gas cylinders blasting through the roof and landing on the road below, some of the cylinders had split open as if easily unzipped and flattened out exposing jagged razor edges. One of these split cylinder takes pride and place at Barnstaple fire station.

Two years after, when I left the Brigade, an existing firefighter told me about a fire in a garage in town in which a car on an inspection lift had caught fire caused by a welding torch. With the car's tyres, fuel, oil, upholstery and plastics burning this would of course produce very dense black smoke which would rapidly fill the workshop area, hang low then make its way out of the large doors at rapid speed. Firefighters in BA were tasked to remain outside of the garage; and with a jet to fight the car fire in defensive mode. The garage staff confirmed to fire crews that there were oxy-acetylene cylinders within the garage, two about half way in and two near the vehicle on fire. With that in mind the OIC ordered the BA crews to take cover behind any solid object, such as walls, whilst cooling down the interior. The two firefighters at the entrance inched forward and struck a large heavy surface area, they could not feel what it was with their heavy duty gloves on, only that it was a heavy chunk of fixed metal of some description; also they could not see it even close up due the intensely thick black smoke. They thought that they now had adequate protection and continued to bravely start to knock most of the fire out that they could see ferociously burning on the inspection lift. Another BA crew were leaning around the outside wall with their jet. They would move in to extinguish and remaining burning material with a dry powder extinguisher. Now that the fire was dying down the smoke began to lift. The BA guys, behind their protective barrier, were now slowly seeing what was shielding them from danger. They looked down and saw what was 'protecting' them, they were kneeling behind two oxy-acetylene cylinders as 'protection'!

SPECIALISTS

I was also an incident command vehicle trained operative. The ICV attends large incidents to assure and maintain safety and command, monitoring the area of risk, monitor firefighters and pumps in attendance, other agencies that may attend and is the main hub for messages to be sent to control and other communications. Being part of the ICV crew we got to see lots of large fires throughout North Devon. All the crew wore red and white chequered tabards, as opposed to the yellow and black tabard of the BACO. These tabards indicated that we were part of the ICV crew and usually a guarantee that officers would leave you alone if they needed hose running out or made up or to wear BA. This was because we were carrying out a specialist task. One operative would walk around the fire-ground collating information and to mark any changes to fire-ground operations, another would be monitoring the radios and receiving faxes and data on the building or chemicals involved, another would be taking care of and amending the Incident Command board, which had all details of appliances and crews and other agencies that were in attendance on the fire-ground. Someone would be keeping a log of messages sent to control and another operative would be drawing a large plan of the whole fire-ground for the fire-ground operative to return and amend it if necessary. Officers could then scrutinise this map and decide if any changes in firefighting strategies are needed. Before we arrive on scene, or on smaller incident when we are not required, (we were normally called out for a five pumps or more) the first pump crew in attendance would take on role of 'Incident command' as all crews have an Incident Control pack from which they can keep tabs on crews and their positions. When the job escalates then we are called to take over the role.

When the ICV arrives, we liaise with the command pump (which should be the only one with blue lights flashing as we can easily identify which crew has taken on the task of control) all other pump's blue lights should be switched off. We then set up, and when we are ready to take over command we inform that pump commander and the Incident commander that we are now ready to take over command at the incident. The pump will then turn off their 'blues' and we will turn on our red and white revolving light on top of our vehicle to indicate where the ICV is situated and that we were up and running. We could also erect an inflatable structure to shield off the elements, lots of officers would gather at the ICV; which can be a hive of activity at times until things were sorted out, calmed down or scaled down. All on-coming crews, Officers and other agencies MUST report to the ICV when they arrive so that we can book them in in case there is a collapse or some other problem so we can track them down with a head count.

I didn't mind being part of the ICV crew, we all used to slot into our own specific tasks to balance up strengths and weaknesses and it worked well. The specialist options on station at the time were the ICV crew or Specialist Rescue Team or SRT.

I wasn't keen hanging from a rope, as the SRT specialises in, and as I had said many of time 'that if I wanted to work from the end of a rope then I would become a climber. My old fashioned stand on these issues were that '*I never joined the Brigade to do things like that, I wanted to fight fire and cut people out of wrecked cars etc.*' But the fire service today is so diverse, it needs to be at times. Oh how the Fire service has changed. Nowadays they train specialist crews in large animal rescues; working closely with Veterinarians on scene. So it was the ICV for me.

MAJOR FIRE

L ots of things go bang at fires when heated. Our Incident Command Unit (ICV) and 022 as support crew pump were called onto a very large twenty pump fire at a large meat processing company, twenty miles away from Ilfracombe. Sunday 13th May 2001. A very major fire was raging within this processing plant in which two hundred and twenty staff were employed. The fire had been raging for most of this Sunday afternoon. The pumps and specialist appliances were being called to the scene throughout the day. We were alerted at around 4pm when the OIC radioed control and requested yet more pumps to the scene. 022 was next in line to be called and were out the doors and on its way to the fire. At 5.15pm control ordered the ICV and support crew. Our support pump had already been called to the incident locally, the ICV was manned initially with a crew of two, a driver and OIC/operator, we would normally take a support pump (022) with back up crew but this had gone and 021 was on an emergency call somewhere in town. We took the station combi-van to follow the ICV. In all fairness the pump for support crew would only be made 'redundant' at a large fire as it was literally used for transport purposes for the ICV support crew only, a van would be suffice and sensible. When we arrived at the plant many fire appliances had gathered and firefighting was well established. Masses of thick black smoke was pluming high up into the clear blue sky contrasting a clear sunny day by a division of a band of thick black ugly smoke. The building was of such a size that firefighting operations had to be sectorised. Sector 1 would be the front of the main building housing the processing element and offices above; and sector 2 would be to the side and rear of the building mainly warehouse and finished plant processes. Further offices which run at right angles to the main building and only attached to it by one end, the remainder of this 'annexe' block jutted out into the end of the car park. I went with Sub officer Williams to get a look at the plan of the building which he had just obtained from a Senior Officer. We stood just inside the main gates, as he opened the plan of the building. I looked about watching various firefighters grappling with jets, an aerial appliance getting to work, BA wearers entering the building and other pumps setting into water supplies. I wondered where 022's crew were, our crew. Strangely I was now thinking that I needed to use the loo! Too much water I sunk down in the station's gym earlier (that's where I was when the call came in). The floor-plan now opened, we went about deciphering the layout. Ben pointed to the rear and side area "Bags, can you look after Sector 2 mate? And get a general gist of what's going on there if you can, also get an idea of what firefighting media is in use, check BA and equipment and who's supplying what with water. Ok?"

"No worries Ben." I said. The job of incident command support is quite straight forward; from this list of work I would also formulate a map of activities that is in full swing outside, such as where the equipment points are, what pumps are supply firefighting operations and where the supply is used from; is it from a river, stream or hydrants etc. How many jets are in use in the area, how many BA are in use in the area, where the BACOs are situated, what officers are in my sector and so on and so forth. This is extremely dynamic and can be forever changing, BA crews change locations or stop wearing, and others enter the building in addition, water supplies change, an aerial ladder is now in use. So it's an on-going monitoring game, but an important one.

"I'll take sector 1 Bags and keep an eye...................." **B A N G.** The ground vibrated extremely violently. The noise from deep within the plant stopped the Sub O mid-sentence, and we both looked towards the building. Nothing indicated a collapse but the BACOs were now busy contacting crews for their welfare state. All were ok and it was reported that from deep within the building that stun cartridges, had exploded from the heat. Thankfully no one was injured and firefighting continued. The smoke plume was reported to be seen from miles around the North Devon area.

I adjusted my red and white tabard and made my way to the side of this vast building. I saw firefighters on the roof of the unaffected parts of the plant also on the office annexe as they poured long pressurised jets of water into the fire that they could see shooting up out of the roof of the main building. Crews had jets going in from ground level also and I noticed, in between the smoke blowing around, the cage of Barnstaple's Bronto being used as a water-tower high over sector 1. To my far left were several forklift trucks which were normally run on bottles of propane gas attached to the rear of these trucks. They were located behind a low wall and had just been spotted by a BA crew who promptly alerted the officer of the sector. I marked the hazards down and confirmed that the officer was now aware of them; I then informed the ICV as regards to this hazard via the radio. Some staff had turned up to watch the fate of their worksite being destroyed and dismantled by the raging flames. According to one of the staff there was another fork-lift truck within the warehouse. The Bronto's branch-man confirmed that the fire was now in that specific area. This area would now need to be evacuated of BA crews and a 'transitional' tactical mode would be put in place; where the fire side of the building could be entered to fight the fire but the hazardous side would have to be fought from outside if possible.. Smoke was billowing from the middle of the plant with intermittent high tongues of flame angrily reaching out of the centre of the building. My sector did not look too bad and slightly unaffected at the time. To the left, just in front of me, was a lorry trailer parked up against the goods-in roller doors; but no tractor unit of any description to shift it. The trailer was known to be void of any products.

I finished my fire-ground plan of sector 2 and personally reported back to the ICV to transfer this information onto the main plan so that any officers may observe the bigger picture from the ICV and make amendments to firefighting operations as they saw fit.

Whilst at the ICV a 'make-up' had just been called for further appliances including another aerial ladder platform (ALP) or Turntable ladder (TL). The next nearest would be fifty miles away at Exeter in East Devon, but this appliance was 'off the run' (either for service or for repair work). The next nearest available ALP was summoned from over seventy miles away from Torquay in South Devon. I headed back to sector 2 which was still a hive of activity. I spoke to a couple of the BA crews which had been inside fighting the fire and was now at the BA area servicing their sets. We had a chat and they described to me the severe conditions within the main building.

My bladder was now screaming "Get me to a toilet…now." We had no formal toilet facilities on the special support units and the likes; so I thought I may have to take advantage of being my own boss in this sector and find a bush, tree or whatever. I'd thought I would better check first though. I found a Station officer (rare occurrence!) who was stood scanning the building. "Boss, have we got any form of toilet on the support pod do you know?" I said, knowing what the response probably would be. He looked at me "No, don't think there is, I went over there." He said whilst he nodded over to the right. I looked over and saw there were no trees, bushes or walls there; only the office annexe with a metal fence to the rear of it. "Where exactly Boss?" This time he pointed, "In there!" he pointed at the annexe itself. That part of the complex was not involved in fire but light smoke-logging had affected the building. I looked at the burning main building which was in the not so far distance, then my eyes went to the first floor of the annexe in which I could see the misty smoke through the windows, then. "Actually IN the building?!" I mused to him in surprise thinking that there may be a chance that he may have been joking. He then replied in a very matter of fact way "Yeah, through the main door, turn left, up the corridor, toilet on the left. I nodded to the Officer "Oh righto.....Ta Boss." in a confused way. He just nodded back and continued scanning the building before walking over to the BA equipment area. I placed my map-board near the BA area and walked purposely over to the building that adjoins with the main plant. The two BA wearers on the roof with a jet glanced down as they notice this firefighter about to enter the building with no equipment. I quickly gave them a nod in a reassuring way as to cause no alarm and that I knew what I was doing; owing to this most significant task that needed desperately to be fulfilled. I pushed through the double wooden doors, turned left and walked through two more double doors then proceeded down the corridor. The building on this ground floor level was quite 'smitchy' with wispy smoke in the air but not intensely smoke-logged as if BA would be required. Halfway down, searching for the toilet sign, I noticed two BA wearers in the mist at the end of the corridor standing at an open fire door with a jet; obviously playing it onto the fire in the adjoining main site nearby, this was where the smoke has entered this building.

They both turned and saw me, minus my BA set, walking through the smoke haze of the corridor. I was not challenged. They nodded to me; I nodded back in return with a smile and entered the toilet. I was stood there doing what needed doing for quite a while, when I inwardly laughed at this ironic situation. Here I am with a major fire going on in the main building in which this building is linked on to, this one is beginning to fill with smoke and I'm stood here urinating formally in a proper urinal in a proper ablution. Surreal.

Once this important duty was finished I left the building; the BA crew at the far end didn't bother to look round. They probably saw the red and white tabard and thought that the ICV crew were a weird bunch anyway.

Just a little over one hour later smoke was emitting through the eaves and cracks of the exterior walls of sector 2. I relayed this change of situation to the Station officer and to the ICV. Firefighting tactics were changed and several jets were trained from the roofs and from the ground onto this sector, a few more pumps had arrived along with Torquay's Bronto (174) this was set up to the right of sector 2, near the 'toilets'! And was got to work as a water tower high above the blaze. I made amendments to my information plan and headed back to check in with the ICV. When walking back I noticed that 2 ground monitors were got to work on the front of the building at sector 1. Ground monitors are apparatus which are placed on the ground and used in place of firefighters. When water is delivered through the monitor it acts in the same way that any large delivery hose would but without anyone actually holding it. The angle of the monitor can be altered as can the spray/jet mode of the branch. These are brought into play if there is a risk of a structural collapse. They play a part of getting water onto a fire but if a building collapses outward then the ground monitor would be damaged without any risk of injury to firefighters. There were obvious signs for a potential collapse at sector 1. As I walked back to the ICV I noticed an Officer, who I vaguely recognised, walking towards sector 2. I recognised him but not from any fire ground before. What rank was he then? I looked at his senior officer's white helmet and saw the large thick 38mm stripe around it. No one has this helmet unless they are the Chief Fire Officer (CFO). Yep, it was him. Unless there was something massive going on (as in this job) we wouldn't normally see the CFO as large incidents as they are usually commanded by other senior officers such as Station Officers, Assistant Divisional officers and Divisional officers. '*Right get into salute mode Bags.*' I thought to myself. Something caught the CFO's eye he then walked towards some pumps which were to his right. Close one.

A quick brew at the ICV (watch that bladder) and a couple bars of chocolate (watch those abs) then I walked back to my sector. 174 was working well before being repositioned as flames were showing at this side of the warehouse.

The fire was ripping through the remainder of the plant with astonishing speed. It really was something else, it had gotten hold and wasn't letting go, almost as if it was on some sort of maniac evil mission of destruction which needed to be achieved. Another ground-shaking BOOM! Another explosion. More batches of cartridges? Or that fork-lift supply inside? Once more I amended the details, I saw more firefighters now working in defensive mode firefighting from outside the building. Fires this large were never normally extinguished by anyone to achieve an effective stop; we just merely tried to slow them down until they relent several hours later; then we could move in and damp down. I looked at the building again to see the framework through the light metal coverings at the end of the warehouse. Everything was spalling (breaking off and breaking apart) and melting devastatingly quick. Through the plans of the processing plant it was now known that the building was construction consisting of metal framework with a brick and block infill which also included sandwich panels. The premises were heavily fire-loaded also. The fire started to burn through the outer skin of these panels; the lorry's trailer then caught light. I looked over to see two hose crews desperately cooling the fork lift trucks and their gas supplies attached. A ground monitor was also used. To the right of the warehouse the walls were disintegrating and decomposing. Within 2 minutes the fire burned through this wall and the far right side was also affected in the same way. Sector 2 was now lost and the whole of the building now involved in fire, save part of the office annexe on the extreme right. Jets were being trained from every angle. Pumps that were supplying the water were lined up along the main road outside the main gates. These were relaying water from either our self-made Brigade dams, lifted from a local stream, or from many hydrants.

Several firefighters that were taking a breather from firefighting were reporting back to their colleagues, who were pump operating, that the place was, in Brigade parlance, "Going like the clappers" Several hours had past and the time was now 9pm. Relief crews were being called in to take over from the earlier pump crews from the initial attendance. The ICV, aerial and other support crews stay until late at night; even through the early hours. A hydrocarbons and fire investigation dog was now at the scene. '*CAPPA*' was a fire detection dog eager to do his bit but it would be a while before his handler puts CAP's special fire booties on his paws in order for him to enter the building to go sniffing. Through most of the early evening and night various parts of the building did inevitably collapse. Just over one hundred Firefighters were in attendance. As crews were very slowly scaled down the building was still showing some signs of fire and severely smouldering all of the next day. It was several days until the Brigade could officially declare that the fire was extinguished.

When the incident finally started to scale down the last formal 'stop' message was sent to control at 23.59hrs devised from the CFO which was as follows:

"......Stop. A building 80m x 40m consisting of 2 floors used as a meat processing plant,

90% of the main structure severely damaged by fire, 2 aerial monitors and 1 ground monitor, 4 jets, 10 breathing apparatus now in use".

After a thorough and painstaking investigation by Fire Investigators (Including 'Cappa') and the Police, it was found that an electrical fault in a sterilisation area of the plant was the cause of the fire.

As mentioned, Station life had changed slightly by the formation of An Incident Command Vehicle/unit (ICV) which attended fires and major incidents and took control over a scene by several people who were trained in this specialist control and communications unit including myself. We would cover the whole of North Devon and saw many a major fires. Also on station we had a Specialist Rescue Team (SRT) this team were devised in North Devon by our Station Officer at the time, Station officer Hale. This team were trained in rope rescues; and were required to either carry out rescues from high ledges or deep wells and quarries etc. Normally these rescues would be in other areas out of our station ground. An SRT team were also set up at Station 4.8. Camel's Head in Plymouth. Each of their whole-time watches were trained as SRT Operatives apart from their White watch who were not. If they were on duty and an SRT call came in which required an SRT, then Ilfracombe SRT would be sent for. Normally local crews had rescued the distressed party before our SRT were in attendance at the scene. Despite training very hard most of the time on receiving a call the team only used to get a few hundred metres from the station only to be sent back as they weren't required. I used to joke as regards to the team turning round and coming back to station and started to refer to them as not the SRT but RTS – Return to Stations.

We were sometimes called to 'make-ups' on other patches other than our station's ground. Schools, restaurants, hotels, factories, thatched premises, these all required several pumps for either manpower, BA or other operational purposes such as operational support and incident command. 022 were called in as 'relief' crew to a large factory that made (or did) furniture at Barnstaple, thirteen miles from Ilfracombe. The initial call was around 09.30am – 10.00am. It took twenty minutes for the fire to rip through this furniture manufacturers building from one end to the other, although fire crews saved a large part of finished goods and documentation stores department. 021's crew were called early on in the initial make–up. We as the crew of 022 got called to the incident at 4pm to relieve crews that had been working at the scene all day.

We worked alongside the Barnstaple retained crew who were damping down with jets, the interior was just one unsegregated area of fallen roof, debris and twisted metal as the roof-beams and pillars were heated to five hundred degrees-plus and fallen in their crazy twisted shapes. I started chatting to a friend which I was at training school with, Rod from Station 01, whilst playing jets on the still hot contents. As we damped down I looked behind me to see a Fire Investigation Officer (FIO) an Assistant Divisional Officer, had moved in and was testing random material by taking a cigarette lighter to it and watching the fire behaviour of the material as it burned, then blowing it out or throwing it to the ground and extinguishing with a hosereel. I said to Rod as I nodded in the direction of the FIO "Aye up mate, what's he up to?" knowingly. Rod looked across at the FIO as he picks up a piece of foam and sets light to it. Rod turned back and continued to train his jet onto the hotspots and out of the corner of his mouth said "There's us trying to put the fire out and that silly sod's trying to start it again!"

STEEP RESCUE

"0 71, 021, 022 - *RTC- LORRY DOWN EMBANKMENT- PERSON TRAPPED- COMBE MARTIN"* Three miles to the east of Ilfracombe, is a village called Combe Martin, a long village which at the east of the village are a series of tight bends. If a vehicle took these bends to fast, braked to harshly or generally lost control they could hit the wall and rebound off it and end up through a small wall and down a very steep wooded embankment. This actually happened to a lorry. The lorry was a skip lorry which, fortunately, had no skip attached at the time. The lorry driver had lost control on one of the bends crashed through a low wall and preceded, cab first, to hurtle down the embankment only to be stopped going all the way down to the bottom of this steep valley by colliding with a tree at the bottom of this deep wooded ravine. Combe Martin's pump (071) was in attendance with Sub officer Coloton in charge. He requested an Ambulance and the Police. Control also alerted Ilfracombe's crews to attend. 07's crew were looking over the edge of the embankment where the low wall used to be when we turned up, we joined them and our eyes followed a long crushed path of vegetation, bushes and branches terminating at the front of a skip lorry which would normally carry waste metals in its skip which thankfully was not part of its load today. The estimated drop from the road to the lorry was approximately one hundred feet. Sub officer Derrin suggested we called the SRT – 02S (S for sierra, phonetically) for assistance to retrieve the driver. We could see the driver moving so we knew for now that he was conscious and breathing. We started to set up lines tied off on the large heavy surrounding trees and the appliances to at least gain access to the driver to check on his injuries and condition. Two of 07's firefighters rigged and descend the drop to reach the driver, occasionally battling through bushes and low lying branches; they removed a large amount of loose wood to make access for the SRT team. After having a chat with the driver they radioed up to the OIC "Sub, just had a chat with the gent, he's obviously shaken but has very minor cuts and bruises, not trapped at all." *very lucky fella* I thought. Up top we had all the kit out that we might have required for the pursuing rescue. The 02S was now in attendance and parked their long wheel-based Land rover widthways across the road where the front of the land rover was facing the embankment, this was so that they could use the powerful winch attached to the front of the vehicle. This could be utilised much quicker than setting up our tirfor winches that we carried and they were hand-operated by pull/push action of the handle. The SRT's winch was fully automatic. The team started to rig their harnesses; they had already changed into their dark blue line rescue overalls back at station prior to mobilising. Sub officer Coloton briefed the SRT "Alright guys, one male driver, conscious and breathing, minor cuts and bruises and not physically trapped. A few of our guys are down there. Safest method to bring him up is by our troll (stretcher) ok?"

The team acknowledged this and prepared to lower on the winch with the troll stretcher. The skip lorry looked unstable and there was a large stream just below the lorry. The order was given to secure the lorry and the Team to descend. The Ambulance crew was now in attendance and prepared their stretcher and Ambulance in receipt of the casualty. We chatted with them, mentioning the condition of their patient and how very lucky he was. Very slowly, due to mechanism of the impact to protect C-spine, a longboard was slid behind the casualty as he was manoeuvred out of the cab and carefully placed on the *troll* stretcher and quickly secured with straps and headblocks. Slowly the casualty was winched up the embankment flanked by some firefighters and placed on the road surface to be checked over by the Ambulance crew we assisted wheeling the driver to the Ambulance ready to be conveyed to hospital. In which he was discharged later that day. The whole operation at this incident took an hour and a half. An RTC where no extrication equipment used in such a tricky and dangerous situation. The driver was a very lucky man.

CHEMICALS

C hemical Protection suits (CPS) and Gas Tight Suits (GTS) were used quite few and far between in the North Devon area. But these suits were essential and had a right of place on the appliances because if they were required they would become second to none in protection against dangerous and noxious substances. My ex-training officer looked at his recruits who looked daunted at the prospect of donning these cumbersome hot suits in the event of a chemical incident. He said "Chemicals.......best thing to do with chemicals? Is bloody well stay away from them!" I thought what a brilliant and logical idea, which wasn't an option for a budding firefighter in training and beyond. CPS and GTS were made up of some very strong rubber-like material, a long way from the old 'splash-suits' in which firefighters used to don a rubber suit then place their boots back on, snap a hood over their heads, don the BA set, their face would be covered by the BA facemask and then the attire completed when their helmet was perched on top of their hooded head. On each appliance we had two CPS. On the old Emergency Tenders, (now incident support units) the GTS were stored. These suits were worn in conjunction with BA sets as the suits enveloped the whole firefighter and fire kit. You would, with assistance, place your legs (without shoes) into the suit, pull it up to your waist, clip the waist-hooks onto your BA waist strap to stop the suit falling down, then the suit would be pulled over your BA set, your head and fire helmet and the whole suit was zipped up via a long diagonal zip at the front. We could see out through a large flexi-transparent aperture which accommodated the upper third of the front of the suit. Lots of safety policies and procedures were in place for the donning, working and removal of these suits owing to the dangerous chemicals that we may have been working with. Zips had to be scrubbed before removal of the suit and it all had to be folded down by rolling it inside out as we removed it as not to be contaminated if any 'nasties' that may have been present on the suit.

One murky-looking Monday morning, just after 9am, we received an unusual shout that 021, 022 and 02C (ICV) turned out to...

'Lorry hit flats-chemicals involved.' Several officers were being dispatched or already en-route to the scene as we could hear over the main-scheme radio. 021 rounded a sweeping bend to see the long sloping road in front of us. A few by-standers there were talking but no lorry was seen. We're waved down. "Down the road lads, over there, over the railing!" the member of public seemed shocked as his concerned face indicated to us that this definitely wasn't a false alarm. We pulled down further and saw a crushed railing and the upper floors of the rear of the flats that were located on the lower road of an estate, the lower floors of the flats to the rear were obscured as they were low down behind a steep grass bank which dropped down to the rear of other properties and could only be seen if you walked over to the pavement and looked down.

As we dismounted from the pump we heard the sirens of 022 and the ICV approaching. Sub officer Williams was in charge of this incident initially. We all walked over to the site of the upper floors of the flats then saw the crushed railing, then the sight that took our breaths away. A large 17.5 tonne, six-wheeler lorry had left the road, crushed the street railing, went over the rail and embedded itself into the lower and middle areas of the landings and kitchen areas of the flats of two building below us. A large hole was evident in the building around the lorry's cab which was wedged fast. This was now declared a major incident especially when we were told, via data and the lorry driver who was out of the cab, that we were dealing with a lorry carrying three types of chemicals, they were, **Hydrochloric acid, Caustic soda** and **Ammonia** which were separated by bulkheads to prevent them mixing together. On further information we were informed that two of these chemicals COULD NOT MIX as if they did would cause an extremely catastrophic situation. Ben called for a make-up immediately and tried to establish if there were anyone in the buildings trapped or hurt. We had the driver with us, so we knew he was safe. A radio message now ordered to all on-coming appliances and specialist vehicles to approach from the west side of town via Lee down. 161, 051 and 071 were in attendance followed by 011, 012, 014, and the Incident Support Unit with several senior officers and obviously the Police and Ambulance Service. Crews had gone down into the affected road to gain access into the flats to ascertain if anyone was trapped or injured. Four persons were found suffering from shock but after an extensive search fire crews had liaised with all occupants at home and reported no injuries. A large part of the lorry and a part of a lamp post were reported coming to rest inside the kitchens of the building. The lorry had fallen approximately sixteen feet down the steep bank. Although the residents were ok they were still not safe. The next consideration was an evacuation of the area, a two hundred metre exclusion zone was set in place and one hundred and seventy five properties were evacuated and these persons were found temporary accommodation at local hotels and halls until the operation was over and the scene safe.

The next questions were how stable were the chemicals? How stable was the lorry? And how stable were the buildings? A Hazardous materials (HAZMAT) Officer was on route to the scene, a structural engineer was alerted along with gas and electricity engineers and the Environmental agency. Data on chemicals was being transmitted to the ICV by fax to advise on what the chemicals were and what measures were to take as regards to safety to all concerned.

As a fire and rescue service, we rigged up in CPS and were briefed on the removal of chemicals and to report any leaks. Due to the angle of the lorry actually bridging a substantial drop, it would prove difficult for crews to access the cab and retrieve the 'Tremcard', this document has all the data on the chemicals carried in transit. We now had to rely on the information from the driver (who may know very little to what is being carried, apart from it can be hazardous.) and information from the Haz-data and Hazmat officer who had just arrived. A Station officer was now OIC on-scene and liaised with the Hazmat Officer.

Other firefighters were setting out a decontamination area, dirty and clean area on the road using salvage sheets water sprays, cloths and had designated operatives to read off decontamination instruction procedure cards to the CPS crews as they removed their suits when they came away from the 'Hot zone'. These cards were in place so that we literally followed the procedures by the book as we could not afford to miss anything in this crucial decontamination phase. In short, the order of the day (and night) was for crews to don up and remove as much of the drummed chemical from the lorry as SAFELY as they could. Some stabilising kit such as winches was set up to the lorry, which was well embedded into the buildings. We now knew that the lorry was as stable as it could be. We awaited word from the structural engineer to offer us the stability status of the actual buildings, 'not too clever by the looks of it.' And we still had these chemicals to deal with. Throughout the morning all of us had worked hard, some of us right up to our limit of twenty minutes in BA and CPS sweating heavily as the drums of chemicals were slowly removed to a safe distance away from other chemicals. We had a break whilst others entered the hot zone, we change our BA cylinders, collected a clean CP suit and done it all again. More pumps were called in to augment the supply of CPS as wearers from all crews were entering the lorry, sometimes four at a time working to shift the load. Information came back that the building would be unstable once the vehicle was moved away from it. And from a chemical perspective was that if two of the chemicals mixed in large quantities then that could go bang kissing the arses of us and an ample part of the buildings goodbye.

I was absolutely *leaking* with the full on exertion and I hadn't really taken that last statement in fully. It was now afternoon and our team were called out of the lorry on a 'time-up' strategy. There were fire crews everywhere. An hour later I, being an ICV operator, was summoned away from CPS operations and asked to 'man' the ICV with the rest of its crew.

I always felt a little disappointed when asked to partake in IC work when I originally started firefighting or in this case humping chemicals around. If we (ICV crew) were on a shout on another stations ground then we were solely just an ICV crew and nothing else. When on our own patch we might start off riding the pumps and after a bit of manual work the designated ICV trained operators were sought to assist run the unit. I always tried to mingle when I was firefighting, head down with the others so not to be dragged away, but they always seemed to seek me, and other operatives, out.

Several officers were discussing further tactics in the large inflatable IC structure when they immediately stopped talking in receipt of a radio message from one of the crews in the hot zone

"............from Team 6. We have just discovered a leak within the container but not spreading through the bulkhead, all drums now removed from this compartment, over." This wasn't great news; we could not afford to have a leak of any sort at this point. We found out that Caustic soda and ammonia can present major respiratory health problems if allowed to mix as this forms a chlorine gas and could lead to suffocation and worse. The leak was absorbed with absorbing agent and correctly disposed of. GTS was now ordered into play.

These were also strong suits which, pretty much, deter anything. So the yellow CPS was now slowly replaced at scene with our red GTS. These were limited and we had to call in our support vehicles from elsewhere to collect and bring these special suits to the scene as far away as South Devon. All through that day and that night and part of the following day all the drums were eventually removed and segregated and made safe for transport away from the site, the scene was scaled down and a heavy-duty crane attended to lift the empty lorry out of and away from the building which was deemed structurally unsafe. The buildings then passed to local building engineers to sort out. How did this all happen to initiate a major incident? The driver (who was a trained chemical transport driver) was a new employee to the company and the area. The driver pulled the lorry in at the side of the road which was on a slight camber over to the right on a brow of the hill overlooking the long road in front of it and the flats all the way down on the right hand side opposite. The driver saw people on the other side of the road, pulled over to ask for directions, he jumped out of the cab and jogged across to obtain directions as they were talking to him they notice the lorry making its own way down the hill, by the time the driver turned around and gave chase to try to jump back into the cab it had become too dangerous to do so as the lorry had built up speed and was heading closer towards the railings opposite. Either the handbrake was not applied fully or there was a handbrake malfunction. An extremely frightening situation for the driver and the residents of this area.

A chemical incident occurred at around 4.30am at a fabrics factory in Barnstaple. Ilfracombe's ICV and support pump (022) both Barnstaple's pumps, their Environmental unit, 051 (Braunton) and 042 (Bideford). The call was to deal with a chemical leak which a security guard making his routine patrol noticed a strong smelling fluid leaking from a twenty five Kilogram chemical drum, which was a quarter full of a chemical which initially was not known to the fire crews. After an hour, with help from the factory managers, which were called in and hazmat data and a hazmat officer; we found out the chemical involved was a highly volatile chemical. The science of dealing with this chemical was very strange. As I was ICV crew I heard and read all the data that came through via fax machine and mains radio-scheme. This chemical was extremely volatile when in contact with water- so we prayed that the skies did not open up. Firefighters in CPS were active by attempting to absorb the liquid then using a putty-like substance to plug the leak. The chemical in the drum was still classed as volatile and it needed to be neutralised before we could leave the scene. So, how do we neutralise it? We sunk the drum in....... WATER.....yes Water!

This is fact and had been advised by our hazmat system, this was checked and double-checked. On the environmental unit we carried large 'over-drums', for placing smaller drums within for sealing and rendering the drum and chemical safe. If we sprayed water on this particular drum with its leaking contents being as volatile as it was it would cause an adverse reaction; but, if we dropped it quickly into an over drum of water this would neutralise the agent, as if we had shocked it into submission. One firefighter, that was donned in a CPS, commandeered the firm's forklift truck and after a crash (not literally) course in the use of the controls the drum was manoeuvred onto a pallet which in turn was then lifted by the forks of the truck and very slowly driven to a field to the rear of the building. Now, waiting in this field was one of our over-drums made steady and filled with water via our hose. All other water kept away. The forklift truck made its way to the over-drum steadied by many CPS-clad firefighters was lowered to the ground. From the pallet strops were attached around the chemical drum, secured and the whole item attached to the vehicle's forks which raised the drum directly over the over-drum. Guided by lines around the drum from a distance the forklift operator gave a call of standby and lowered the forks at a rapid rate swiftly descending the drum into the over-drum of water. The lid was quickly sealed to the result of the chemical now being neutralised with no adverse effect. A rapid cooling affect had possibly played a major part in the stabilisation.

THE DARK ELUSIVE BIN

On a lighter note, 022 was called to a bin on fire at 7.45pm one dark winter's night on the sea front, next to one of our local beaches. We arrived to see a large square waste bin, with an integral cover on it with apertures around each side at the top, the bin's contents was merrily smouldering away. I grabbed the hosereel from the nearside locker and kept a safe distance (not worth risking anything over a bit of rubbish in a bin) I identified the dark outline of the bin on this dark evening and spotted the even darker slots near the top of the bin where the litter is pushed through, the bin was shadowed by the yellow din of the street lights. I blasted a jet of water at one of the apertures. After a few minutes I noticed that the bin was still busily smouldering, so a longer spray jet of water was concentrated at the slotted opening to cool the fire this time a bit nearer and a bit longer, a quick check revealed that it was still on fire. I moved even closer, looked down and saw a large pool of water on the ground below the bin after my efforts to extinguish it. Even if there was a hole in it; it would at least put the bloody fire out. One of the lads walked over near the bin "Try another slot Baggy" I thought that they were all the same! But I hit another slot with the water and moved even closer. Still a large pool of water gathered around the base, and the bin still smouldering badly. My mate inspected the bin, had a feel around the slots and slowly turned to me with a big smile on his face "WHAT?" I said in frustration, he pushed his hand through the top of the opening "Try now Bags" I moved forward with the water on and the smoke was instantly replaced by steam and the fire now extinguished, then I realised that this type of bin had no permanent open slots but these slots had top-hinged spring flaps which needed to be pushed in before depositing rubbish before the flap springs shut on its own. Longest bin fire I had attended.

HIGH STREET PERSON'S REPORTED

E veryone has heard and seen the media's attempts to transfer messages over to members of public as regards to the dangers of fire and smoke. *'Get out, get the fire brigade out, stay out!'* - *'Put it out-right out (as regards to cigarette and pipe smokers) - Smoke kills-think about it! - Know your fire escape plan.* And a leaflet from the mid-80's, a black fire information leaflet which on the front showed a close-up of a 'Fireman's' BA facemask, just seeing the eyes within, with light smoke floating around with the words *'A Fireman has breathing apparatus to survive in smoke-all you have is this leaflet'.*

Today the message states *'Fire Kills!'* Fire and smoke work in conjunction with each other, fire kills yes but smoke also kills and can reach a victim by spreading and seeking out that victim, rendering that person unconscious; followed by death. The smoke stems from fire so as they work hand in hand the statement 'FIRE KILLS' is just that.

A spread of smoke leads me to the next incident.

At 2.40am one Wednesday morning our teleprinter message read *–'FIRE ALARM SOUNDING- SMELL OF BURNING.'* The fire alarm actuating was within small newsagent/confectioners located in our main High Street. 021, 022 and 014 were mobilised and when we turned up and dismounted there was a definite strong smell of burning accompanied by a fire alarm actuating from the building. I was riding as BA 4 on the second pump, 022, so once in attendance I ran out a hosereel and luckily located a fire hydrant quickly and set in to it for the pump operator. Breaking-in tools were being taken from the lockers by the first BA crew. I glanced across to the shop to see a dull orange glow deep within, towards the rear of the shop. The BA crew gained access and smoke immediately poured out into the darkened street. The team entered the smoke-filled building with a hosereel jet and radioed back to the BACO that there was quite a well-established fire in the rear storeroom.

"ANOTHER TWO BA, NOW! AND MAKE PUMPS 4" The OIC demanded across from the road, I jumped into the nearest cab, grabbed the main-scheme radio and made pumps 4. The second crew rigged up and awaited their brief then they entered the premises with a jet that I had just laid out, they then backed up the first crew in firefighting operations. I ran to 021 and used their delivery hose to run out a covering jet. I set up some spotlights and set up an amber light at the BA control point to indicate to crews where to muster first before they went in and when they came out of the building. A spotlight was shone on the floors above the shop.

This was a club that was disused since it has been relocated to new premises elsewhere but; we had been informed that there were flats within the club and was unsure if people lived there. The spotlight showed signs of smoke-spread behind the glass of the club up on the first floor. Most of the club's previous entertainment was held on the first floor. We were still not sure about fire spread as yet. A third BA team had been instructed to enter the building to complete a search of the area; they had also taken a jet up with them just in case. Most of us knew that there was a flat at the top of the stairs as we had carried out a BA exercise in this building several months earlier, but we were unsure of the location of other flats above the club itself there were no other external doors leading up to the flats above from ground level. The rear of the premises was being checked to find a fire escape. The club's entrance was on the ground floor next to the newsagent, you then walked up a long flight of stairs which returned back on itself you then enter the club on the first floor. Up at the top of the stairs was also a flat. "BA control from BA team 3. Flat located and searched, all clear, no sign of fire, continuing search through the bar area - Over?" I glanced behind me and saw the blue flashing strobe lights of Barnstaple's aerial platform arriving. "BA TEAM GET RIGGED!" The OIC, Terry, ordered once again. Me and another firefighter grabbed our sets from 022 and received our brief at the entry control point. The Sub instructed us as we started-up. "I want you to meet up with team 3 and conduct a search as the floor area is quite large. They are on a left-hand search. I want you to go in on a RIGHT hand search and make contact with team 3". We finished climbing the long stairs and entered the bar area, commenced with a right hand search then came across some stairs. We descended the four stairs then entered an open room with a pool table in the middle of it. The smoke wasn't too bad here and we could just about identify objects and make out the layout in the smoggy haze. We came to a door on our right and checked for heat which was not evident then entered the room and checked what seemed to be toilets, all clear; we came back out into the pool room and continued a right hand search. The next door on the right was slightly ajar with a 45mm hose trailing through the gap, we followed the hose down a short corridor then to the left up a wide staircase, the smoke was dense here. "Ere, feed up the hose will ya? We need some more up here." The voice was from one of team 3 crew who were another two floors up. "OK mate, will do, hang on" my mate said as we both retraced our steps back to the door and pulled more hose through until a loop straightened out. We began to heave it up the stairs. Because the staircase had a central built-in column we had to take the heavy hose around this column and up the staircase as opposed to running it up through the middle; which would have been easier.

We met up with team 3 "Alright lads? Where have you searched?" I asked keen to get on. "We've searched the entire floor below, just got these rooms to do." I looked behind me. "Righto, we'll check these rooms you go up ahead then" I said. First room clear, we had to feel around quite a bit now as the smoke was even thicker and use the BA shuffle technique. I wondered how they were getting on with firefighting below in the shop.

We then met up with team 3 again and proceeded to enter the second bedroom, nothing found so far. My mate momentarily left my side and walked over to the bed "Hang on a minute." I followed and strained to see what he looking at; he lowered his hand to feel the mass on the bed.

"OVER HERE FELLAS-CASUALTY" I shouted whilst attempting to shake the form of a gentleman lying on top of the bed. "BA Control from BA team 3, casualty found in a third floor bedroom, standby...." Team 3 relayed the message. I took my glove off and checked the casualty for a pulse whilst my mate was still nudging the guy to see if he could get a response. I stopped as the wiry man groaned and stretched. One of the team 3 guys came over and shouted through his facemask at the guy as I attempted to drag him out of his slumber. "COME ON MATE, WAKE UP, SHIFT YOURSELF. IT'S THE FIRE BRIGADE. WE'VE GOT A FIRE BELOW AND NEED TO GET YOU OUT. NOW! COME ON MOVE YOURSELF." The guy apprehensively got up, with our hasty assistance and we part dragged and part frog-march him down the stairs. "BA Control from BA team 3, casualty conscious and breathing we are bringing him out now." We came out into the street clutching this guy tightly as he was still disorientated and spluttering. An Ambulance had been called and was in attendance. We handed the Gentleman over to them for a check-up and reported to BACO. We informed the BACO that we had found no fire spread on the upper floors but only smoke-logging and all the rooms were now checked. Both our teams were told to shut down. I saw another 2 BA teams from another station that were now rigged and ready to go in. I looked over at the shop to see that smoke was still issuing but looked as if the crews were now starting to damp down. The fresh crews were ordered to go to the upper floors to vent the area of smoke. The aerial appliance had now got to work in order to check the building on the upper floors and roof externally. The Ambulance was still in attendance tending the casualty who more than likely had smoke inhalation but otherwise a very lucky fella. We cleaned and tested our sets and had a look at the fire damage once the smoke cleared. The rear storeroom had a fairly intense fire that had caused smoke-logging to other parts of the building through open internal doors and partitions. The guy we escorted out from the upper floors suffered smoke inhalation (no surprise there then) his outcome was good.....and very lucky. Cause of fire - power surge in electrical system resulting in an electrical arc.

FLASHOVER

"**O**21, 022, 014 - *FLAT FIRE – PERSONS REPORTED.*" It was 3am on a Saturday morning. The call slip was handed to the OIC-Sub Officer Williams in charge of 021, leading firefighter Hunter in charge of 022. I was riding as BACO on 021. The fire was not far from the station again, in the main high street. As we pulled out onto the forecourt I noticed the flashing blue lights of the Ambulance turning out from their station next door as they added the urgency to the turn out for a Persons reported call. We turned right into the high street and that's when we encountered thick smoke hanging all around the area in the street. The next thing we saw was sheets of flame, reaching out approximately ten feet, bursting out of the second floor window of the flat. "Christ, there are people over there under the window on the pavement, look." said the guy riding BA1. 022 pulled up behind us and their crew dealt with the people under the window where the fire was showing. They were huddled round a woman lying on the ground apparently having lowered herself then jumped from the window to escape the fire. The crew, with the help of by-standers, and the Ambulance crew had no choice but to move her to safety out of harm's way. She had no burns but had suffered back injury. The guys riding BA 4 on both pumps ran out firefighting jets and a covering jet whilst the drivers were setting into street hydrants to urgently augment their tank supplies. I set up the Entry control point across the road away from the danger of the leaping flames and falling sparks, embers and debris. I stayed in-sight with the alley that led the crews to the side door to allow them to gain access into the flat. The first BA crew received their brief, booked in with yours truly, and took a jet with them to the second floor. I then checked in a second BA team. As I waited for the third team to get rigged I saw that the Ambulance was just leaving the scene for hospital with the casualty. A jet was being trained on the flame-engulfed window from the street. Number one of the third team confirmed his brief with me, after starting up, handed in his tally and quickly walked towards the alley, not waiting for his mate and not confirming his details with me. His mate came to me, and through masked face he only shouted out his air capacity and in a flash he turned to follow his mate. I grabbed for his BA tally but without success as he had quickly turned to catch up with his number one, not even confirming his full details either; tally still attached to his set, which was supposed to be with me. This is basic paramount BA procedures and they had just shunned this. I called after him, amongst all the noise and melee with the pumps screaming, people shouting and the noise of the fire. I tried to call before he entered the alley and out of sight, he may have forgotten with the adrenaline rush, but they SHOULD NEVER forget to carry out proper procedure, especially whilst working in BA.

"OI, MARTY, MARTY GET BACK HERE!" My shouts fell on deaf ears. I radioed them. "BA team 3 from BACO, YOU RECEIVING OVER?" a pause........

........"Go ahead BA control."

"TEAM 3 YOU MUST RETURN TO BACO - YOU MUST BOTH RETURN TO BACO...NOW OVER."

They only got as far as the far end of the alley and not as far as entering the building.

In BA you carry out work in two's so you go in together and come out together. The team didn't get very far and walked over to me. I pointed to Marty "You, Tally, Now; and confirm your air pressure" I was a little pissed off with his lax in procedure. He confirmed his details handed me his tally, I checked his gauge then his mate looked at me "Why did you call us back out, that's dangerous." I stared at him wildly. "I'll tell you what's bloody dangerous MATE, is one, leaving your BA team mate behind and two, not handing in your tallies and three not getting your kit checked properly THAT'S what's bloody well dangerous." The operation at the scene was not compromised in anyway as a BA teams had now entered the building and was working to good effect. Team 3 re-entered the alley, the number one grumbled something or other, I wasn't concerned what he thought but I knew I was the person who would be keeping a close check on them and get him out of the nasty stuff if push came to shove. I was doing my job and they should have been doing theirs correctly. We'll see later.........

Two teams of BA wearers walked urgently over to me and started up, following procedure they then entered the burning building, they were followed by Leading firefighter Hunter "Bags, we just heard from one of them lot" he pointed to a few of the bystanders "That there may be kids up there, as they have not, apparently, been accounted for. We've made pumps, and these 4 wearers have had their brief and going in to search and rescue." The teams that stood next to him in readiness quickly and concisely confirmed their brief, followed entry control procedure then entered the alley to locate the door to climb the external concrete staircase to search for the missing persons. By this time I was itching for a 'wear' and get in there, but I could see that everyone on the fireground was busy with their own jobs and the officers were busy commanding the scene and wouldn't want me badgering them just so I could have a wear. Anyway it was crucial that I stayed managing the board as I could fully oversee what each crew was doing and where they were at this critical time. Progress messages from the teams were being passed back to me but the hard work up there had not as yet paid off as regards to locating the missing persons. I could only imagine the conditions they were working in as I had been in those circumstances and will be in many more to come.

A 1.3.5. Ladder was now slipped and pitched over a builders skip to the second floor as the flames had now been knocked back into the flat.

Then a stark garbled radio message, almost panicky came over my radio "............mergency..........firefight........trap. I repea...............!"

I strained to listen harder to the radio, what's he saying for Christ's sake?"

"This is BA control, repeat your last" I then pressed the radio up to my ear and blocked my other ear with my hand to drown out the background noise. Then I heard it. '*OH GOD. Sounds like a firefighter in trouble.*'

"BA TEAM 3 TO BACO – BA EMERGENCY – FIREFIGHTGER TRAPPED, FIREFIGHTER TRAPPED – DSU ACTUATED, OVER."

I acknowledged the team and told them that I was preparing to send in an emergency team. I asked for further updates when possible. I shouted for the Sub officer and the Leading firefighter, I relayed this message and I got sent two BA wearers ready to go in and ascertain what exactly was going on and to assist the distressed wearer. On main-scheme radio the emergency procedure was swinging into place. My heart was now pounding like a drum.

Any firefighter could inform control about the BA emergency at this incident and they in turn would automatically call for extra appliances, an Ambulance, a senior officer, and a BA instructor to investigate the BA used at the incident. I could just about hear the DSU sounding and getting louder and louder and was relieved to hear that the firefighter was located and the others were safe. The emergency team had entered the alleyway. The flames seemed to be appearing at the large window opening once more. Something's not right up there as they *did* have the fire under control. Word came back to me that the firefighter that was in trouble was Marty (Mart, who didn't or forgot to hand his tally in earlier) he witnessed a flashover; in which the flames rapidly made their way up the corridor that the crew were proceeding, Shane (No1) hit the deck and due to the heat, air pressure and confusion Marty was thrown into a room; the door slamming hard shut behind him. This happened so quickly that Mart did not know what had happened. One minute he saw flame the next he was in a different compartment, full of smoke and pitch black without his BA partner and desperately searching a way to get out by groping for a door or window. The others shouldered the door and grabbed mart and got him out.

The DSU sounded louder as Marty was escorted out of the building by Shane and the emergency team, the other firefighters were now firefighting again on the second and now third floors. Mart walked over to me looked shaken ready to collect his tally. "Mate, look at me, you ok?" I said concerned at his shaken demeanour.

"Phew, yeah I think I'm ok Bags, bloody hell mate."

"I'd get your set off mate, have a drink and have a break for a bit" I told him.

Shane grabbed his arm. "Yeah, come on mate."

I handed Shane his tally "You ok mate?" I asked.

"Yeah, went all a bit mad up there. Flashover" he said.

I passed him his tally. "Aye I know. I'll get one of the officers over to check on you both."

Sub officer Williams walked over towards me, I pointed out that the BA crew were behind me servicing their sets. Ben had a chat with them whilst they had a drink during the set checks. I saw the crew change their cylinders for full ones. After checking a team out and another in I was aware of another team rigged ready to go in.

A brief was given and I looked up for their confirmation and saw it was Marty and Shane again. Mart was obviously extremely shaky when he came out prior, but now he was stood at the Control board ready to go back in. (Well, if you fall of your horse..........)

"You ok mate? Both of you ok for this?" I asked them both as they were a team and were in there together. "I'm alright bags, just need to get back in there. Sorry about before mate, here's my tally" Mart said a little bit sheepishly as he handed me his tally with a shaky hand. I didn't say to him that 'that that was ok and forget it'; as it wasn't, and these procedures were had to be strictly adhered to for a purpose which could save their lives, especially when their safety also depends on my awareness and actions as well as themselves. This was proven on this incident. "FF Peters, 280Bar, time in at 03.25hrs" I checked his tally details and air pressure then checked Shane's details and let them continue their search and rescue. After obtaining progress reports from the crews I heard reports of no persons found. All other occupants of the other flats had been, or were in the process of being evacuated. The whole of the flat and the building as a whole had been searched thoroughly, checked and re-checked to no avail. Some of the crews had withdrawn to say that they can honestly state that they had searched every inch of the place and had not found anyone. People do strange things in the event of a fire, especially children. Some will hide in wardrobes or under blankets, under beds or in cupboards to escape smoke and flames. Some people will try to escape but collapse near their escape route; so would collapse behind doors or under windows.

That is why firefighters are trained to spread out and check ALL of these places then check again. Within ten minutes word came to the officers on the fire-ground that the children were never inside the building and were actually staying with family safe and well somewhere else in town. What a massive relief that was. A lot of energy was asked from the crews to search for these individuals.

Remaining BA crews were told to stand down their search but continue with assisting with firefighting. A message to control over the main-scheme radio was sent stating that all persons were accounted for, and probably a telephone call, to control explaining the situation. I was finally relieved from BA Entry control. I asked if I could have a wear which was granted and I checked in correctly at BA control along with another firefighter from our crew and entered the building to fight what fire was showing inside. From the previous intense fire the initial entry into the flat was now showing as a very ugly black tunnel. We checked for any hotspots and re-kindling in this area. We checked the room to our left, this was the room Mart had become trapped and disorientated in, quite smoky but no fire, the room opposite, just up the hall, had signs of hotspots so we knocked them out with the hosereel that we had grabbed just inside the main front door. As we continued down the hall we came across another crew in the lounge dealing a small fire in the corner of the room. We passed them and check a bedroom to the left and extinguish a small fire in there. The atmosphere was still filled with irritating smoke.

Me and my team-mate withdrew from the building to collect some kit for turning over, cutting out and dampening down such as axes, jemmy-bars, shovels and the likes and re-entered to spend a good forty five minutes on this task. Daylight was upon us and pumps and specialist appliances were scaled down. Three pumps remained as the building was still vulnerable and hot. BA was now scaled down and withdrawn completely as the smoke cleared through natural ventilation. BA was replaced by normal fibre protection masks whilst we cut away floorboards and lathe and plaster to prepare for a full fire check. We were working with a few of the lads in the kitchen area. This area was still extremely hot and hotspots everywhere. Axes and jemmies were used to remove charred wood and a cool spray from the tubing soon extinguished all the remaining hot spots. Now at full daylight at 8.15hrs it was looking to be a nice day out there as I glanced briefly out from the blackened hole which was the second floor window. We all mustered in the blackened shell of the lounge and started to rip up old bits of burnt and smouldering carpet and threw it carefully out of the window into the builders skip which was conveniently in place below. The lighting that had originally been brought up through the night still picked up severely smouldering areas of the room which were dealt with before being removed from the building. We had to make sure that all materials were fully extinguished as we did not want the fire starting up again when we left the scene OR get called to a skip on fire below! The third pump now returned to their home station leaving just 021 and 022 crew at the scene.

When we stepped outside for a drink, rest or ciggie; the sweat on our bodies started doing its job; to cool us down. In the clear air outside I found myself feeling quite cold after the exertions upstairs as the sweat evaporated on the body when not active, steam hazily dispersing from fire kit in the summer light. It almost seemed a joy to get back in to the hot rooms to turn over and damp down again to warm up once more. Crews left the scene at 11am that Saturday morning and the High street turned back into some normality for the shoppers and traders and Fire Investigation Officers and Police now started their painstaking tasks.

The female occupant apparently had suffered several vertebral fractures of the spine. We had a spate of 'persons reported' calls strangely seemed all at one time, almost like these, other calls came in clusters like the RTC's, false fire alarm calls and malicious hoax calls.

We had entered several buildings throughout a two week period and rescued several persons from fire and smoke. Several, as mentioned previously, were oblivious to fire dangers through alcohol, when the inebriated left food to smoulder on the cooker as they fall asleep. Fire safety messages were always being broadcast to members of public via the media as regards to safety and personal responsibility. Some 'persons reported' jobs were through genuine electrical malfunctions or accidental cause. Normally in the early hours of them morning. People still need to check and double check that electrical equipment is switched off, cigarettes and other smoking materials were extinguished – properly; and cookers and gas hobs were correctly turned off before retiring at night.

A COLLECTION OF THE BIG ONES!

We did get the 'big ones' mainly hotels. Such hotels were usually derelict. The Brigade have had several of these derelict buildings burnt out such as the 'Candar hotel' and arcade fire (1983), this (occupied) hotel took up a large part of upper fore street with it. Next to the hotel was a large walkway capped off with a glass arched roof which led from the high street to the sea front/promenade area. There were shops and burger sellers down either side of the walkway (I can still smell the onions frying now as I write) I digress once more. This fire started in the early hours of the morning and resulted in a few injuries and a hotel worker losing his life after an explosion within the building, other guests only had the clothes that they stood up in as they had lost everything to the flames. This fire required twenty pumps to extinguish it.

The derelict 'Beacon Castle hotel' (1985), located high up on a hill and fanned by the winds from the Bristol channel resulting in the building, that was well alight prior to the brigade arriving on-scene in the early hours, literally razed to the ground, just a blackened shell of the ground floor was all that remained as dawn broke the following morning.

The 'Runnacleave hotel' (1988) saw Firemen fighting a severe fire from 10pm one Sunday evening. The fire was first witnessed emitting from a flat roof, but was internally apparently taking hold rapidly resulting in the west side of the building gutted despite an eleven pump attendance.

The derelict 'Mount Hotel' This building 'went up' one Wednesday afternoon (1992) during the annual local rescue demonstration on the pier near the harbour that always attracted holidaymakers and locals alike.

A spectator at the rescue event was chatting with fire crews; then with a look of surprise and confusion pointed up the pall of black smoke that had just started funnelling from the top of the derelict hotel up on a hill above the town, and said to Stoney with shaded eyes from the sun "Oh is that part of the rescue demonstration?" Stoney turned round to witnesses the scene high up on the hill; equally surprised he turned back to the spectator and said "Ah......NO!" All the appliances that were at the pier then abandoned the rescue demonstration very quickly and headed out of the pier gates in urgent convoy and up to the disused hotel that was severely damaged by fire.

As mentioned previously in this book, the Derelict Cliffe Hydro Hotel had us attending several times. The old hotel is now demolished, a very plush elderly person's sheltered accommodation was built in its place. A fantastic new building complete with integral car park, still with the sea views and overlooking the harbour.

The 'Hotel Cecil' (2002) which was having a refurbishment had a fire break out within. The Fire Service were alerted at 8pm. Fire was evident on all floors of the building and firefighting efforts internally were hampered by the refurbishment work that had been going on inside. The flames started to break through the large ply wood boards temporarily attached to the large windows along the front façade of the building and the flames had also smashed the large window on the first floor above the entrance. A small steeply ascending alley allowed us to access the rear of the building. Inside it was reported that firefighters in BA had entered a narrow glass-enclosed staircase to reach the first floor when the glass had actually melted and in one sheet flopped over out of its frame onto the firefighters, this was simply pushed off and they continued their task. This concluded as an eleven pump fire.

A large derelict Amusement arcade (2004) near the sea front was reported to be on fire by members of the public at around 8am. On our arrival the building was well alight, and firefighting took all day which was then reported as an asbestos risk. Some of us returned at 4.30am the next day to continue to damp down and provide a spray to keep asbestos dust down whilst mechanical demolition equipment was used to demolish the whole building. Now demolished nothing has replaced the building on site at the time of writing.

A very seriously large fire at another derelict Hotel saw this being over twenty pumps and other specialist appliances. The 'Montebello Hotel' fire (2006) caused damage to other surrounding buildings including part of a roof of a residential home in the road behind the hotel. Twenty homes including the residential home were evacuated. The hotel itself was located in fore street, just down the road from the Candar hotel which was gutted by fire in 1983. Whilst firefighting to the rear of the hotel from Portland Street I experienced a surreal atmosphere that of a scene around me in the streets, similar to the effects of the 9/11 attacks on the Twin Towers of New York, but on a far lesser scale.

The whole road leading into the High street and fore street was covered in thick grey dust which had caked buildings, vehicles, roads and pavement alike. Ash was continuously falling around us. Flames punched twenty feet into the air accompanied with the usual crackling and popping with the odd explosion. Pumps and other appliances as far away as Sidmouth and Torquay in South Devon attended the fire. The five story hotel, needless to say, was totally destroyed and demolished later. At time of writing no other building has replaced this.

The derelict 'Berkley hotel' (2007) received an eight pump attendance for smoke issuing at approximately 7pm one evening. Firefighters used BA to fight most of the fire internally in offensive mode, due to the unsafe floors operations were switched to transient mode in which BA could be used partly in the building but also be fought from outside.

The splendid Collingwood hotel (May 2007), Derelict at the time of the fire. The gable end and rear of this building were severely damaged by fire and collapse. (See below) Other major fires and incidents were attended on other station grounds also, not just in Ilfracombe.

A building of splendour was located on the corner of Wilder road on the sea front at Ilfracombe. A majestic regal-looking hotel called The Collingwood Hotel. This hotel was very popular to holidaymakers and local organisations alike, holding dinner and dances, weddings and corporate events within this glamorous building. The Collingwood was a large white building of five floors (the fifth floor being part attic rooms). A small visitor car park was to the front. A tea shop and hotel bar adjoined to it at ground floor level, this bar was known as 'The Edwardian bar', a relaxing lounge bar favoured by residents and local public. Beyond this bar heading to the rear of the hotel was another bar, 'The Vaults'; also a very cosy but spacious area where many a disco and other functions had been held in the past. The vaults bar was impressive with its large open fireplace and thick cavern-like pillars randomly situated around the room. Further to the right of the hotel outside was an adjoining conservatory which led into the main building up into the guest's rooms. Over time this hotel unfortunately ceased business and fell derelict. It, however, kept up its clean appearance exteriorly, but the rooms inside were now partially damp and falling into disrepair. The Collingwood had been shut down and derelict for many years; a dreadful shame to all that were acquainted to her. Would this be the last episode of her fate?

THE GRAND COLLIE

O n a dull drizzly bank holiday Sunday morning in May 2007, we all received a rude awakening from our Sunday lie-ins to respond to the Collingwood hotel to reports of '*SMOKE ISSUING – FIRE*' The time was 08.30am. Due to the number of calls (multiple calls) the aerial bronto, 014 and Woolacombe 161, were ordered on to assist both our pumps. I was riding 021 as the spare man, BA4. We could smell the smoke from nearly the other side of town. The miserable drizzle and heavy air was supressing the smoke layer as it drifted laterally. As we neared the hotel the smoke was thicker and reaching right across the road. I jumped out and scanned the building to see no obvious flame showing on the floors of the façade of the building; Lots of smoke was evidently billowing from the roof area which looked as if it was from the rear of the hotel. One of the OIC's (I cannot remember who) came running down the side road and ordered most of us who had just dismounted the appliances to run out a 45mm and a 70mm jet and get them to work at the rear gable end of the building, accessed by a small path. Once the hose lines were coupled together four of us dragged the lines to the rear of the building and radioed back for water on. I could feel the heat from the fire as we entered the small path and on looking up at the rear of the hotel saw an awesome sight; flames were bursting out of several windows from the first floor to the top floor. A good quarter of the building was well alight. We held fast by digging a bight of hose into the wall behind and leaning heavily on the charged 70mm hose to counteract the pressure velocity as it kicked out hundreds of litres of water into the building.

The branch-men next to us proceeded further up the path and played water in through the other end as to stop the spread to the rest of the building to prohibit it creating a major inferno involving the whole of the ex-hotel. This seemed to work very well and we remained in the area firefighting for an hour before being relieved by other crews. After a quick brew Matt and I reported to the OIC for another tasking. One of the ADO's wanted BA crews to carefully enter the building to knock out any deep-seated fire that was encountered on the ground floor to the rear of the building. Myself and Matt were tasked to don BA and enter the building via the conservatory to the right of the main hotel. This had to be broken into to gain access; so we grabbed some breaking in tools and forced the door using two swift blows with a sledgehammer. A hosereel was laid out already to take in with us. Once the door was forced we entered the conservatory, headed left through the main hotel door which led us to the ground floor rooms. The first three doors were tested for heat and smoke, none present. They were then cautiously opened, no fire. We then knelt outside the fourth door and tested it for heat and smoke. No smoke emitting from around it but definitely heat detected.

We gave the surface of the door a quick spray from the hosereel to see how far the flames were heating it up on the other side by observing the steam level on the door's surface.

The door was steaming halfway down. We decided to crack the door and give the room a quick drink as well as taking advantage of a quick look to see what was going on in the room whilst keeping low. After the door was opened and a two second blast from the reel, a quick look and the door was slammed closed again. I could see that there was a well-established fire in the middle and right side of the room. The door was opened again, I kept the branch open and whilst on our knees keeping low we attacked the fire knocking it back to the outer walls. The bed was alight but didn't take us long to extinguish it. I gave my mate the branch to knock out the remainder of visual flame; I checked the bathroom and second bedroom to our left. I was only two metres away from Matt and still had him in view. The door frames were severely scorched but otherwise untouched. I disregard these and headed back to him. We made sure the fire was out then proceeded to check the other rooms along the corridor, some fire damage was discovered in the next room but others, so far, unscathed. Matt sent back a 'sitrep' to the BACO and we were then asked to withdraw. We met another station's crew that had made their way in to assist us; we told them that the ground floor this side was covered and now clear of fire. Outside we grabbed a brew, cleaned and checked our sets and replaced the empty cylinder with a full one. Whilst chatting I noticed that the main hotel door was open exposing the reception area, foyer and the large elaborate grand-staircase ahead. BA wearers were called for; so Matt and I stepped up for another tasking. A Station officer had just briefed the Sub officer, the Sub then headed towards us "Right then you two, I want you to go up to the third and fourth floors, via the main staircase, make your way to the third floor and check all the along the far right corridor for signs of fire. Then make your way to the fourth floor and carry out the same task, ok?" Matt repeated the brief in confirmation. The Sub pointed into the hotel "Two teams have just been committed to search the ground, first and second floors, you may see them later. Take a hosereel in with you. Report to BACO." then he was gone to command another sector.

After explaining our brief to BACO we entered the grand main staircase and proceeded up the stairs to the upper floors with the hosereel in tow. This main area was smoke-free and clear as day so we hastily made good progress to the upper floors. We passed a BA crew checking rooms to our left down a corridor toward the rear of the hotel on the second floor. Only then was it that I realised that the main fire alarm was still sounding; I'd been so caught up in the escalating incident. The fire alarm sounding were caused by the working detectors heads still operating in the derelict hotel setting off the fire alarms. As we reached the third floor smoke was swirling and becoming denser as we approached the corridor leading from the middle to the rear of the building. We began checking the area. There was neither fire nor evidence of previous fires within the corridor; however, there were some debris around.

On looking around I saw that some of the ceiling had been damage, maybe through collapse above. We then came across a room on fire and spent some time fighting the flames back, we then moved on and extinguished another fire in the next room which we contained.

Just then I heard an almighty crash in another part of the hotel, it sounded quite near but we witnessed no collapse or felt no movement. I looked up to see a weird lattice pattern embedded in the room's ceiling. I pointed upwards alerting Matt. "What's that?" I said to him. He shrugged his shoulders "Dunno, looks like a bed base and frame" I looked at it for a few seconds more then realised that it was the bed frame from the room above; it had burnt its way down through the floor joists, that had more than likely been alight in the room above and burnt through, and came to rest on the floor and was burning merrily into the ceiling above us. I immediately alerted BACO to make sure that the OIC was aware as BA crews may be entering these rooms above where floors were obviously weakened. The alarm bells were annoying me now. I grabbed one of the hotel's fire extinguishers off the wall hooks and took a swing at the bell situated high on the wall. The bell was quite high and I am not the tallest of people; so I just caught it enough to distort it which changed its sound from a very loud and fast **ring-a –ling- a- ling** to a dull mute-like dig-a-dig-a-dig. On checking more of the corridor we also had a couple of rooms to check at the far end. The smoke was thicker now, floating around us. Another ringing bell, I turned to Matt who was six foot tall; I placed a fire extinguisher in front of him "Ere you are mate, you're a long thing, sort that bloody thing out will you?!" I said fed up with the constant ear bombardment. I saw his eyes crease as he broke a smile behind his facemask. He did the honours with a direct hit and stopped the ringing.

The next room had the door ajar; there was a smouldering heap on the floor with evidence that that room had been alight but looked like a jet from outside had knocked it out. We dampened it down and proceeded to the last room right where the fire was at its most intense. I noticed a communal bathroom on the other side of the corridor and at the end of the corridor noticed the fire escape door open which led onto the external fire escape. Had it been open all along or had fire crews forced it to gain entry or to vent from the inside? Moving on I checked the last door and opened it. I cautiously stuck my head round and looked into the room; I had just taken a step in and stopped immediately, frozen. "WHOA! SHIT, LOOK AT THIS!!" I shouted to Matt through my facemask and opened the door wide enough to let him see (I don't know why I had to do that as I bet he was look right over my head seeing what I saw straight away) "SHIT!" he said in obvious reply to what he had just mentally taken in. Ahead of us was half a room; Yes literally half a room, partially burnt and the remainder missing, gone, no more. The whole outside of the room, floor, windows and the entire outside wall had completely collapsed to the ground below outside. This confirmed the loud crashing sound earlier what we heard just along the corridor. I reckoned three or four paces and we could just step off a floorboard and plummet to the ground.

I was shocked, eyes wide open while I slowly looked out to the area outside to the rear and saw a few firefighters waving at us. The whole upper third and fourth floors on this side of the corridor had collapsed. I waved back at the crews, shrugged my shoulders and we retreated from the 'room'.

Matt relayed a message to the OIC via BACO as regards to the collapse and danger on these upper floors. In reply we were informed that the Officers were aware of the situation and they wanted us outside. We retreated down the main staircase and saw another two crews withdrawing via the staircase also. I didn't recall hearing an evacuation whistle. Maybe due to the collapse being at the far end crews were probably evacuated via the radios. A Sub officer came over to us whilst we reported to the BACO. "Right lads, well done, clean and service your sets and get a brew and a bite to eat, the chippy's open just up the road and they're catering for us" the Sub said. I removed my facemask and whilst doing I said to the Station officer walking by "Did anyone sound for a evacuation boss?" he continued to walk by half turning when I saw a radio clamped to his right ear; obviously listening out to a conversation to the radio and not fully hearing my question. Never mind, we got our sets serviced then made haste to the chippy, we were starving. The drizzle had now turned to heavier rain fall. The brigade's 'handyman/driver' had been to the fire-ground and delivered some light frame work which had been erected and a salvage sheet placed over it and tied in place as to protect the crews who were either taking a rest or servicing sets. The BACO threw over two bottles of water for us. I looked around and noticed that officers had scaled the incident down. There was now no obvious flame just a smoking roof, hot spots and a scorched hot building to the rear. I saw other fire crews removing a hose from the main building, others, were servicing sets, others are making up hose. I saw a hose-line snaking up the side road to the rear of the hotel where I could hear it working, being trained onto the burnt and now water sodden building.

Others were tucking into fish and chips; some were at the Incident command vehicle parked opposite across the road, along with a few Officers. I spotted two Ambulance Paramedics eating food and drinking tea whilst standing-by for the firefighters on the fire-ground. A quick task was called for. This was for a couple of BA wearers to open a few fire doors at the far end of the hotel at the side of the building to ventilate the smoke and to let the firefighters in to damp down.

Again, Matt and I both rigged into BA and open the fire doors where the communal bathrooms were. We opened each door on every floor (the top floor was opened, as it transpired, by a crew earlier in that area before re-tasking). We were met by a crew walking up the fire escape at the fourth floor level and told us that their brief was to damp down. We let them pass and now our simple task was done we decided that we may as well take the fire escape down to ground level and report back to the BACO. After a full damping down BA all was discontinued.

The bronto could now use a jet from above with no risk to injuring crews. 014 had now got to work as a water tower aiming a jet down into the building from high above. Me and Mart and a few others decided to sit at the tables back in the Fish and chip shop rather than sit on the wall opposite the fire site. No members of public were in there, as there were not many around on this murky grey late Sunday morning. We all sat there, blackened, dirty faces and hands smeared by carbon from the fire, drenched bodies feeling uncomfortable, forking chips in to our mouths in an uncivilised way. The owner of the fish and chip shop was an absolute star for opening up and serving a bunch of, now stinking firefighters. We all appreciated his charity of free fish and chips. Makes you appreciate the great spirit of the good people of the Town. I saw more firefighters had come in; after fifteen minutes of break comprising of food, cuppa and a sit down we decided to get back to the fire-ground and let them have a break. Firefighters were now rolling hose, making up hosereels, returning equipment and tools back onto the pumps. The jet round the back was still working in conjunction with the bronto's monitor, so to avoid being 'dicked' for a boring making up task. I sneaked passed some officers in discussion and jogged up through the path that leads to the rear of the building to see how the crew on the jet were doing. They were a crew from Combe-Martin and they were happy giving the building its last drink. We had a quick chat and decided to get stuck in with last of the making-up after all. The incident was now scaled down to one pump (021) and the bronto. After five hours the incident was wrapped up and this once splendid building was left in partial collapse looking a very sorry state.

One fire call in which I did not attend but was told about (I forget by whom); amused me so much I had to include in the book. It was a call to a fire alarm sounding that was from a building of multiple occupancy, they were flats. The call was made by a young Spanish man. After his own quick investigation to what and why these alarm bells were reverberating the building that he realised that it was a fire alarm but could not see any signs of fire nor smell burning. He called 999 then run down three flights of stairs, stopping momentarily for a second on each landing whilst he descended to meet the brigade in the street. On the crews arrival, the frantic lad who was speaking to them with a good attempt in broken English, pointed to the wall where the bells were located then covered his ears in a *'bloody noise!'* type way. They walked into the premises amongst the loud ringing, but kept the alarm going to assure that others within were aware of the need to evacuate. More people came out of their flats, but only when they saw two fire engines outside, and not before! They were as equally confused. They were escorted into the street as the crew conducted a thorough search of the flats that we could gain access to fire opening the unlocked doors civilly. A search revealed that one of the occupants had been over-zealous with the cooking which was the cause of the alarm but was oblivious to the thick smoke on which the firefighters were 'chewing!' So they turned the hob off, removed the smouldering pan and vented the flat completely. They then met the OIC at the fire alarm panel back on the ground floor. He had just silenced the alarms then went to reset the whole system once the smoke had cleared. In theory, if the panel was silenced then reset but it immediately sounded automatically again this could mean; a) they hadn't done a good enough job on venting the smoke! b) There was a fire elsewhere in the premises or c) there was a fault with the system (which normally would show up). This panel had a zoned LED area which showed red on the first floor, the affected flat, so if it went off again we would have gone back to option A. The panel did reset nicely, and so they had the task of checking the area. A firefighter said that he stopped half way up the stairs and walked back down to the ground floor "Break-glass gone here." He said whilst inspecting the split in the aperture of manual alarm system. You would physically push the glass aperture with your finger, the glass would split and push the button behind it and in turn would cause the alarm to sound through this manual method. Some thought it great fun to push these and call us out on a false alarm. I prefer a few beers in the pub for fun myself! But there we go. Anyway they replaced the glass panel, when someone heard another voice. "Another one gone up here." From the first floor, then a distant voice "....and up here." They found that every manual break-glass alarm was pressed and actuated throughout the whole building. They thought someone was having a laugh. They told the remainder of the occupants that all was clear and asked them if they knew why all the break glasses were set off. The Spanish lad pushed through to the front to speak to them "I push, I push" he said whilst rein-acting a pushing type finger movement. The OIC looked at him "you push them all yes?" the lad nodded excitedly in agreement. He then expressed "didn't work." Pointing to the break glass again. All the firefighters were confused.

The L/FF piped up again, "What didn't work?" The lad looked frustrated. "The bell, I push, didn't stop, then tried others, still no." the L/FF looked at his crew "AH! Right." And put his thumb up to the lad who was now just as confused as they were. The L/FF laughed "You know what he's done? He thought that these were to STOP the alarms, not set them off! So he bounded down the stairs and pressed everyone of then on each landing! Classic." The L/FF then explained what the break glass alarms were actually for and how they worked and both crews left the scene with wide grins on their faces.

Several years after the above incident we attended that same building (nope not the same lad) for a *'fire alarm sounding-smell of burning'* one Saturday evening at around 10pm. I was riding our first appliance 021 with 022 in hot pursuit of us. L/FF Mcgovern and myself were donned in BA and as we stepped off the pump there were occupants mingling outside of the building, an evident noisy alarm ringing and now smoke issuing as well from a first window that was ajar. One of the flat's occupants approached L/FF Stone, who was our OIC, and mentioned that there was a cooker on fire.

Stoney briefed us and Stevie and I traipsed up the first floor flat armed with a hosereel and a DP Extinguisher. The door to the flat was on the latch, we entered a very smoke filled hall which led to a very smoke-filled kitchen; in fact the whole flat was smoke-logged as all the doors were left open. We both approached the cooker but saw no flame, but a lot of hot smouldering material on and inside the cooker. It looked like the occupant had definitely overcooked whatever culinary dish it was. The cooker was still on. So I turned it off, whilst Steve gave the area a quick drink from the hosereel then I went and open the window in the kitchen and other rooms. The flat was completely smoke-logged to the point that we were feeling around the place. I opened the lounge window wider and saw that L/FF Hunter's crew had two BA ready. They wasn't required at this point. One of the firefighters was administering oxygen to one of the occupants who probably had smoke inhalation and possibly shock.

Back in the flat we managed to prise some of the hard congealed material off the cooker including a smouldering hot saucepan and removed it to open air outside of the main door. Back at the upstairs it was still smoke-logged but was clearing very slowly, visibility was still down. I felt my way through into a bedroom and opened the window and turned to see Steve disappearing through the smoke into another room to the left. I opened another small window then turned round to see Steve opposite me. Well, I saw a form standing there in the thick smog but saw his DSU flashing its red light every few seconds. This must have been an adjoining room "Alright mate that was quick. All done?" Steve didn't reply and just stood there looking in my direction as indicated by his flashing DSU light.

"Steve, mate. What's up? You all done?" Still nothing. I walked toward him as he came towards me, I thought he'd gone deaf or had seen something that has shook him up. "Stevie, what the matter mate. He kept coming towards me. I lifted my arm to grab him and I thought that he lifted his to, then I heard a noise to my right by the door. "Sorry Bags, I could hear you talking, I was trying to open a tricky window in there. What did you say mate? You alright?"

"Whoa", I said. "Where did you come from?" I looked back to where I thought he should have been and felt forward in the smoke, that's when I got closer and closer to this other firefighter, and made contact with..........Me! I was talking to myself all along. Well, actually talking to Steve whilst looking at myself all along in a mirror that was fixed to a wardrobe door! Eventually the smoke completely lifted enough for the full-length mirror to show itself. I was joined again by Steve who stood beside me and took a look in the mirror. "Oh yeah, there I am Bags, that's me in there."

We had a good laugh about it, re-checked the cooker and made our way out. An ambulance arrived now to tend to the occupant, 022 had made itself available and was now turning down the road to head back to station. The OIC gave some safety advice to the occupant, and we made up and returned to station also. I was telling the crew about the mirror incident. And was surprised to hear that at least one of them had or at least heard of other firefighters experiencing this. Smoke plays funny tricks. You just do not want to get lost in it!

A LAST WORD FROM ME....

When my career came to an end in 2009 I looked back on those thirteen years of service with pride of what had been achieved as a team and the closeness of that unit through thick and thin. Whether people trapped by fire or disorientated or overcome by smoke; whether they are at the mercy of rapidly rising flood water or trapped in a vehicle after a collision; you could be rest assured that after that 999 call is made the dedicated highly skilled and committed crews will be on their way to perform an extraordinary job of which many would not or could not do.

I was very proud to serve with Devon and Somerset Fire and Rescue Service. And to those who had served in the past; give yourself a personal accolade and a round of applause for the determined contribution that you gave. For those serving currently and future firefighters; all the very best of luck to you all. You do an outstanding job.

THE END

ABOUT THE AUTHOR

Tony joined the fire service in April 1996 and served thirteen dedicated years in North Devon at the Ilfracombe fire station. After many interesting incidents that he and his colleagues attended over the years, he saw fit to write about his experiences. Tony still lives in North Devon with his family and endeavors to continue writing.